FORT DAVIDSON
AND THE BATTLE
OF PILOT KNOB

FORT DAVIDSON
AND THE BATTLE
OF PILOT KNOB

MISSOURI'S ALAMO

WALTER E. BUSCH

Series Editor Doug Bostick

Charleston   London

THE
History
PRESS

Published by The History Press
Charleston, SC 29403
www.historypress.net

First published 2010

Manufactured in the United States

ISBN 978.1.60949.023.2

Busch, Walter E.
Fort Davidson and Battle of Pilot Knob : Missouri's Alamo / Walter E. Busch.
p. cm.
ISBN 978-1-60949-023-2
1. Pilot Knob, Battle of, Pilot Knob, Mo., 1864. 2. Fort Davidson (Mo.)--History. 3.
Fort Davidson State Historic Site (Pilot Knob, Mo.)--History. 4. Pilot Knob Memorial
Association (Pilot Knob, Mo.)--History. 5. Fortification--Conservation and restoration--
Missouri--Case studies. 6. Historic preservation--Missouri--Case studies. I. Title.
E477.16.B88 2010
973.7'37--dc22
2010029502

Dedicated to a special woman and a carriage ride.

Contents

Preface   9

Acknowledgements   11

Introduction   13

Chapter 1. The Union Army Comes to the Valley   15

Chapter 2. Then Came the Tug of War   27

Chapter 3. The Death of Fort Davidson   33

Chapter 4. Reconstructed...from the Ashes   41

Chapter 5. Tenting on the Old Campground   45

Chapter 6. Where the Cannons Use to Roar   51

Chapter 7. Retelling the Battle: The *Iron County Register*, 1882   59

Chapter 8. Pilot Knob Memorial Association Anniversary Booklets   65

   Meeting of the Pilot Knob Memorial Association (1904)   66

   Second Annual Meeting of the Pilot Knob
         Memorial Association (1905)   92

   Third Annual Meeting of the Pilot Knob
         Memorial Association (1906)   119

CONTENTS

Appendix 1. Troops Known to Have Been in the Arcadia Valley
during the Civil War   157

Appendix 2. Text for Selected Photos   161

Appendix 3. H.R. 4923: A Bill to Create Pilot Knob
National Battlefield   167

Notes   171

Index   187

About the Author   191

Preface

This book began as merely a transcription of the three Pilot Knob Memorial Association books. As you can see, it blossomed into a book unto itself. As research continues, hopefully more information will be uncovered—maybe even enough for another book. It is indeed unfortunate that many of the local papers for that time are gone, as I'm sure that more information could have been gleaned from them. However, this book provided the proofreaders with some fresh information that they did not know, so it should provide you with basic information about Fort Davidson, the Battle of Pilot Knob and the Pilot Knob Memorial Association and its efforts to preserve the site.

Acknowledgements

While not totally comprehensive, I wish to thank the following people who have helped with this project: all of my critical readers who made sure I proved my facts, including Jack Mayes, Brick Autry, Joe Snyder, Chris Warren, Gary Scheel, David Roggensees and others; and Bryce Suderow, author of *Thunder in the Arcadia Valley*, for getting me interested in very large transcription projects. However, most of all I want to thank Dr. Douglas Eiken, former director of Missouri State Parks, and Gary Walrath, my former supervisor, both of whom had enough faith to hire a former police sergeant to run a historic site.

Introduction

In the dark of the cool, damp early morning about 3:00 a.m., blinding light flashed continually across the sky, followed by a large explosion and then many smaller ones. More than twenty thousand pounds of black powder had flashed and burned, throwing timbers, dead bodies and lead shot high into the air. The deafening sound could be heard for twenty miles. The powder magazine inside Fort Davidson had exploded, killing all of the Union soldiers—or so the Rebels believed.

The next morning, General Sterling Price discovered that the enemy had slipped out of the fort. He sent one-third of his soldiers chasing after the escaping Union soldiers under General Thomas Ewing through the St. Francois mountains and Ozark hills. Some of the Rebels remained behind to gather supplies in town and bury the dead in the rifle pits of the fort.

Here ends the story of Fort Davidson, at least as far as any major military actions are concerned. What follows is the rest of the story. While Fort Davidson suffered some misuses over the years, such as serving as a corral for mules and oxen, the old fort was never forgotten by the men who fought in it. Indeed, many men of the 47th and 50th Missouri Infantry and the 3rd Missouri State Militia Cavalry, as well as many citizens and former soldiers in the 68th Enrolled Missouri Militia who fought there, passed by the fort field on a regular basis. To them, it was always something to remember and memorialize.

Had it been a battlefield far away, such as around Nashville, where the 47th later served, the burning desire many had to memorialize this field would not have existed. Men from the 14ᵗʰ Iowa Infantry who fought here were interested in memorializing this field, but they had also fought at Shiloh and in the Red River campaign. Many battlefields drew their interest to commemorate their deeds.

Largely it was local civilians and soldiers who defended Fort Davidson. Men who, in their old age, desired to see it set aside as more than a field owned by a mining company—a field where people would gather after church to picnic, play games and search for artifacts from the battle. Fort Davidson had been the focal point of their battle, their glory and their Civil War, and they wanted to make sure that their story was not forgotten.

The story of Fort Davidson is more than the battle. It is more than the stories of the men who served and fought here, which are preserved in Cyrus Peterson's *Pilot Knob: Thermopylae of the West* or in the Peterson Collection at the Missouri Historical Society.[1] It is the story of the Pilot Knob Memorial Association, which was formed by the survivors of the battle to preserve the fort. The story is found in the records of their association, some of which are provided here; in court records at the Iron County Courthouse; and in newspaper accounts and surviving photographs. The story continues from the time the association finally purchased the land through the twentieth century until, near the end of that century, its dream was finally realized when Fort Davidson became a state historic site. It continues to this day, as site personnel write plans to preserve this fort for future generations.

Here is the story of Fort Davidson, told in the words of the survivor's association and newspapers, but before we get to that, a summary of the fort's history is in order.

Chapter 1

The Union Army Comes to the Valley

F ort Davidson was not the first fort in the Arcadia Valley. Beginning late in 1861, the soldiers of the 33rd Illinois built an earthen fort on the hillside overlooking the junction of the road to Pilot Knob and the Fredericktown road, inside what is now Arcadia. They christened it Fort Hovey, after their commander, Colonel Charles E. Hovey[2], and it was officially recognized as such by Special Order No. 15, dated October 6, 1861, issued at Ironton by Colonel W.P. Carlin.[3]

The January 1, 1862 edition of the *Normal Picket*, a newspaper written by soldiers from Normal, Illinois, while they were stationed in the valley, described the almost completed fort:

> *It is not true that the rifled cannon are to be mounted* in place *of the present large smooth-bores; but* in addition *to them. Nor is it a fact that the larger excavation in the rock, west of the fort, is merely to be used as a mine, to be sprung in case of necessity. It is to be used as a Magazine; and will immediately receive the heavy supply of fixed ammunition now at Pilot Knob. The small tunnel connecting it with the fort is merely a means of communication. The mines are not in the close vicinity of the fort at all; and are only connected with it by the electric wire.*
>
> *The supply of water from the artesian well is also, perhaps, over estimated; though we are assured it is amply sufficient. On this subject, however, the engineers say there will be no trouble, as the depth of the boring is so slight that it will only require a few hours to enlarge the caliber, if found necessary.*

As to the fort itself…its oak and earthen walls are capable of resisting very heavy shot, even at short ranges. The banquette [a platform inside of a parapet, for soldiers to stand on when firing], *now complete is capable of accommodating two regiments of infantry at once; and the bastions are so arranged as not only to enable each gun to sweep all the angles which relate to its own bastion, but* three-fourths of the guns can be brought to bear at once upon any point.

For the past week, all persons except such as have duties in the fort have been excluded. But it is known that the bomb-proof barracks are nearly complete; and that all the appointments for offense and defense are nearly ready for service.

It is estimated that the fort (with its surroundings) is impregnable to any force which can be brought against it, without the facilities of rail-road or river transportation.[4]

Iron ore production was the main reason for the construction of Fort Davidson. *Missouri Department of Natural Resources Fort Davidson Collection, #L65-2004-002-0004.*

The Union Army Comes to the Valley

During January 1862, soldiers poured into the Arcadia Valley, probably as many as 2,500.[5] The Ironton post bakery was issuing an average of 1,061 loaves of bread per day, each weighing forty-four ounces. Meanwhile, in Pilot Knob, members of the 38th Illinois were complaining that they wished they had cabins instead of the Sibley tents, "a tall round [conical] structure, large enough to accommodate twelve or fifteen men," with stoves in the center of them.[6] Also in January, the 24th Illinois Regiment, which was overseeing the construction of Fort Hovey, had completed its main work, and the unit left to rejoin its regiment in Kentucky.[7] This fort remained the only earthen fort in the valley until 1863 and, after the Battle of Pea Ridge, Arkansas, was renamed for General Samuel Curtis.

Fort Curtis, like Fort Davidson would become, was a defensible position only against small guerrilla units and small cavalry formations. It was never meant to house 2,500 soldiers for long periods of time. Soldiers threw up tents and shanties in the fields near the fort, in Ironton and in Pilot Knob. Some lived in local houses and inns, paying rent. In the valley, Sibley and other tents remained the norm for a soldier, but eventually barracks were erected for both soldiers and freed African Americans who worked for the military.[8]

Military life followed a fairly strict schedule, as the "General Calls at this Post" directed:

Early war view of iron production at Pilot Knob from *Frank Leslie's Illustrated Newspaper* September 7, 1861, page 260. *Missouri Department of Natural Resources Fort Davidson Collection, #65-2008-004-0001.*

Camp Blood, located on the north side of Shepherd Mountain, from *Harper's Weekly*, September 21, 1861, page 596. *Author's Collection.*

Reveille	*5:30 a.m.*
Breakfast	*7:00*
Surgeon's call	*7:30*
Guard Mounting	*8:00*
Company Drill	*9:00*
Drill Recall	*11:00*
Dinner	*12:00*
First Sergeant's call	*1:30 p.m.*
Battalion Drill	*2:00*
Drill Recall	*4:00*
Dress Parade	*5:00*
Supper	*5:15*
Tattoo	*8:00*
Taps	*8:30* [9]

The Union Army Comes to the Valley

Fort Curtis protected the southern approach to the valley, but it was defiladed from the south by a nearby hill that was within small cannon range. In January 1863, Colonel John B. Gray, commander of the post at Pilot Knob, reported to the assistant adjutant general in St. Louis that Fort Curtis had four thirty-two-pounders and two twenty-four-pound howitzers. Still, three days later, he commented in another letter that the fort was useless and recommended abandonment.[10] The fort was "useless" because these big guns did not protect what was truly important to the military and the reason the Union originally put soldiers in the valley in the first place: the iron deposits and railroad.

The north end of the Arcadia Valley had two mountains, Shepherd and Pilot Knob, upon which high-quality iron ore had been found. The quality of the ore was such that because of these two mountains and nearby Iron Mountain, one of the first railroads coming out of St. Louis, Missouri, passed by the arsenal, Jefferson Barracks, and ended at Pilot Knob. America's wartime economy needed iron ore for more railroads and for manufacturing. The St. Louis and Iron Mountain Railroad delivered the valley's iron to St. Louis and the rest of the nation.

When the Civil War broke out, the Union needed to protect its supply of iron and the railroad terminus, so troops quickly occupied the valley. One of the first regiments to garrison it was the 21st Illinois Infantry, led by Colonel Ulysses S. Grant.[11] The valley became a jumping-off point for Union military operations in northern Arkansas. It was only a few days' march to Crowley's Ridge, which was the high ground, extending for miles, in swampy southeast Missouri and deep into Arkansas. Union operations in Rebel Arkansas were made easier by traveling down the Iron Mountain Railroad to Pilot Knob and then taking military wagon trains south through Patterson over to Bloomfield to reach Crowley's Ridge and Batesville or directly south to reach Pocahontas, Arkansas, on the mountain road.

As the Union supply depot, Pilot Knob also became an organizational center of Union activities in the local area. Companies of Union soldiers garrisoned outposts at Centerville and Barnesville (Ellington) in Reynolds County; Glover and Arcadia in Iron County; and Patterson in Wayne County. Patterson and Centerville were considered permanent outposts of the command at Pilot Knob. The Knob, as it was often called, also served St. Francois and Madison Counties and the Iron Mountain Railroad at least as far north as Cadet station in Washington County. By October 1862, there were "about seven thousand soldiers here" and "six pieces of artillery" recently arrived from St. Louis, according to Private John Kelsey, company

Left: Early war graphic of Brigadier General U.S. Grant. *Digital Photo Collection, Library of Congress. Call no. LC-USZ62-110716.*

Below: *Arcadia Valley Views by Perkins*, a turn-of-the-century drawing of the spot where Colonel Grant received his general's commission. *Missouri Department of Natural Resources Fort Davidson Collection, #65-2002-023-0001.*

G, 24th Missouri Infantry. Campaigning into northern Arkansas had begun, and the Knob was serving as a deployment camp.[12]

Early in the war, Missouri State Guard general M. Jeff Thompson bypassed a fortified Pilot Knob and attacked units of the 33rd Illinois along the Iron Mountain Railroad at Blackwater bridge over the Big River in northern Washington County. By April 1863, Confederate raids were more heavily armed, and an attack on Pilot Knob became a distinct possibility when General John S. Marmaduke raided into southeastern Missouri. On April 22, the colonel commanding Pilot Knob wrote to General Davidson that "[i]f we are not attacked tonight, I feel I can assure you the enemy will get no supplies from here" and then asked permission to abandon Fort Curtis, as he believed it could not be held.[13] Fortunately, events near Cape Girardeau forced Marmaduke to shift his raid in that direction and away from Pilot Knob. Despite its armaments of three thirty-two-pounder siege

Old soldier at the spring where General Grant received his commission. Postcard. *Courtesy of Charles Brook.*

21

General William P. Carlin, 38th Illinois Infantry, commanding at Pilot Knob; he also fought at the local Battle of Fredericktown in 1861. *Digital Photo Collection, Library of Congress. Call no. LC-DIG-cwpb-06853.*

guns, two Coehorn mortars and three twenty-four-pounder howitzers, the commanders felt that Fort Curtis was useless.[14]

Early in 1863, the Union district command decided to build another earthen redoubt in the field south of Pilot Knob. Pilot Knob was closer to the iron mines and the railroad, the sinews of war that needed to be protected. Unfortunately, no position in the valley was a perfect site. Almost anywhere north of Ironton Gap, a nearby mountain easily defiladed a potential fort. Putting a fort atop the mountainsides (although it was later tried on Rock Mountain) made little sense for long-term siege warfare, because of three reasons. First, the water supplies were lacking on the surrounding mountains. Secondly, rock made a poor building material subject to shattering and sending additional projects at defenders when struck by cannon fire.[15] Dirt, on the other hand, allowed for softer impacts, which would imbed solid shot and not add more flying projectiles to exploding shells. Finally, and most importantly, improperly placed cannons on heights cannot be depressed to fire once the attackers pass a certain point. They are then "under the gun," which is a safety zone.

A fort in the plain also made better sense because the Union commanders were certain that the Confederates could only throw infantry and cavalry at them. When General John Sappington Marmaduke raided to Springfield and later Cape Girardeau in 1863, he brought infantry and cavalry. During the fall of 1863, Colonel J.O. Shelby raided up to Marshall, Missouri. He brought only cavalry. The fort, therefore, only had to protect soldiers against a few small field cannons brought by a cavalry striking force. If a fort's armaments included several large and mid-size cannons, they could easily outgun any defilading cannons, which, if placed on any of the surrounding hills, could not be protected from fire from the fort. What the Union felt it needed, and what it built, was designed as a refuge from such forces and so designed that they could hold out for several days. That is what they started building in 1863.

According to Major Robert L. Lindsay, Fort Davidson was "named after a man for whom the people of South-East Missouri have very little respect."[16] It was built on the plain north of Ironton Gap between Shepherd Mountain to the south and west, Pilot Knob Mountain on the east and Rock Mountain and Cedar Mountain to the north and northwest, respectively. The east and west branches of Knob Creek provided water. Troops had already been tenting on the plain since the late 1861. Now they began to construct a fort within cannon shot of Ironton Gap.

From the fall of 1862 to June 6, 1863, Brigadier General John Wynn Davidson commanded the St. Louis district of Missouri, then the Army of Southeast Missouri and then the St. Louis district again. During this time, he busily supported General Steele's campaign against Little Rock and kept troops moving through Pilot Knob. Davidson, a career soldier, served in the army before and after the Civil War. Why a citizen-soldier like Lindsay would not like a man like Davidson is not difficult to understand.

During Davidson's tenure in these posts, the military began constructing the fort bearing his name. During the next several months, the 1st Nebraska, the 3rd Colorado, the 3rd Missouri Cavalry, prisoners and contrabands (runaway slaves working for the army) built the fort.[17] Wanting the fort finished quickly, the post commander, Colonel R.R. Livingston, ordered all able-bodied men to work on it. This included not only enlisted men found outside of their quarters after taps but also civilians and contraband. Livingston's action brought about a complaint from Major Lindsay, an officer in the local militia, that "a precedent has never been made in this war where loyal citizens have been ordered under penalty."[18] The order was rescinded; however, people of contraband were still employed, some of whom were pressed into service from the employ of local citizens.[19]

The engineers—with Second Lieutenant Fred Smith, 1st Nebraska Cavalry, in charge of the on-site construction—designed the fort as a six-sided structure of fifty-one thousand square feet with ramparts. Over the hot, sweltering summer, soldiers, prisoners and the local "African Phalanx" worked on the dirt fort. In the July heat, the regimental quartermaster of the 1st Nebraska issued one barrel of whiskey for the men working on the fortifications. Each man received half a cup each day.[20]

By September 1863, General Clinton Fisk advised his commander that the new fort was very near completion.[21] On February 27, 1864, the chief engineer of the Department of Missouri, Captain William Hoelcke, reported on his inspection of the new fort:

> *I have the honor to return rolls. &c., of negroes employed at Pilot Knob, Mo., for building fortifications at that place. The work done by the negroes is a regular hexagon redoubt of 140 feet for one front, consequently with a fire-line of 840 feet; the whole mass of earth (rather a little rocky) dug out and filled up is about 150,000 cubic feet. It will take a regular organized force of 220 men (the number of negroes employed and accounted for on the rolls) about twenty days to finish the redoubt, while the negroes, according to the rolls, have been working about seventy days in average. But considering all other circumstances, erecting a rifle-pit of 750 feet in length, excavating a well of 50 feet depth, digging a large powder magazine, erecting an extensive stockade around the prison, &c., I think it just to pay the negroes so usefully and advantageously employed. I never received any reports as to the employment of the negroes; only the fact that a fort had been erected at Pilot Knob was known to me, and therefore I cannot approve and testify any of these rolls.[22]*

Many years after the war, Sergeant Henry C. Wilkinson described the fort in a letter to Dr. Cyrus Peterson, who was preparing to write a book about the battle:

> *Fort Davidson was hexagonal and each side 40 yards long, or 240 yards around and 80 yards across. There was a sally port on the south side, just aside from the head of the south rifle pit. So in going into the fort you stepped into the heavy door of the sally port and you were then directly*

under the south parapet and then to your left was a stair way. On going up the stair way, you emerged through a trap door into the fort. On the east side, facing the old Pilot Knob Ry. Depot, was the gate way with a heavy draw bridge that hinged to heavy timbers at the gate entrance. Then with windlasses inside, attached to high strong posts, this bridge was drawn up by means of ropes extending from the windlasses up over pulleys at the tops of the posts, then attached to the outer corners of the bridge.

Fort Davidson then mounted four 32 pound siege pieces or pivot guns, some 12 or 14 feet long, and if we remember rightly, they weighed 9000 pounds.

Then there were three 24 pound howitzers, with limbers so they could be hauled on the field, some as field pieces, as heavy field artillery. Also there were two mortars about the same caliber as the 24 pound howitzers. As we have read several descriptions of the old fort and its surroundings, we will now add our mite, of its position and surroundings. So now we will stand in Fort Davidson and look around. The fort stands on the point of a very high ridge or roll of land, which extended south from Cedar Mt., on the north, to Stout's [Knob] Creek which flows from the northwest. Looking westward, there is a mountain something over a mile away, which bears away to the southwest. Extending from the fort to this mountain is a rolling flat or plateau of low ridges or rolls. Also these rolls were covered more or less with bushes.[23]

When completed, the original fort proper included a south rifle pit that extended to the west branch of Knob Creek, about 150 yards south of the fort. The fort also stood higher in the plain than did Ironton Gap and commanded it with its guns. The terrain sloped gradually at a fifteen-degree incline from the fort down to the gap.[24] The north rifle pit was built later. This was earthworks now known as Fort Davidson; however, the military post at Pilot Knob included buildings throughout the entire Arcadia Valley.

Military buildings around the Pilot Knob area included a military telegraph office and quartermaster and commissary stores, all probably located near the railroad terminus east of town; two buildings within a stockade, serving as a guardhouse near the modern-day junction of McCune and Mulberry Streets in Pilot Knob; stables, some apparently located east of town and some near the area of the guardhouses; and barracks to house some soldiers and the freedmen located probably east of town near the base of Pilot Knob Mountain. A smallpox hospital in Middlebrook, just north of Pilot Knob on the Iron Mountain Railroad, also served the post.[25] The main hospital that could hold up to two hundred men was at the Ironton House Hotel, about half a mile south of Ironton Gap. Numerous picket posts also served the military post by policing the local populace and warning of guerrilla operations. The most prominent one was a picket post atop Pilot Knob Mountain. With its commanding 360-degree view, large troop movements could be seen as soon as they entered the valley through almost any gap.[26]

Soldiers would camp out on the fields surrounding Fort Davidson. Many had tents or small huts in the area west of the fort along the base of Shepherd Mountain that had been known officially as Camp Herron but popularly as Camp Blood in 1861.[27] Other locations included pickets near the Russellville road junction with the Fredericktown road and at every railroad bridge between DeSoto and Pilot Knob.

In late summer 1864, the Union military had definitely fewer than two thousand men camped in the Pilot Knob–Arcadia area, as many troops had been transferred from Missouri to support Grant and Sherman in their eastern operations. Local men formed Company "E" of the newly formed 47th Missouri Infantry and camped across from the courthouse, while the 3rd Missouri State Militia Cavalry camped farther east around the area now known as Buckey Court. Others camped around Fort Davidson and the still active, but less used, Fort Curtis. As the summer progressed, more and more rumors began to spread that Confederate major general Sterling Price was on his way to seize the state for the Confederacy. In preparation, Brigadier General Thomas Ewing Jr., commander of the District of St. Louis, ordered the clearing off of "all trees on the hillsides within long rifle range of Fort Davidson, and to thoroughly block up all roads leading to any of the hills which are within range of ordinary field artillery."[28]

Chapter 2

Then Came the Tug of War

The Fort was always conceded to be indefensible against any large army having serviceable artillery. Early last summer, I sent competent engineers to select another site, but such are the difficulties of the position no practicable place could be found any more defensible. I therefore had the roads leading up the hills obstructed, cleared the nearest hill sides of timber, and put the Fort in a thorough state of defence by deepening the ditches, strengthening the parapet, and adding two rifle pits leading north and south commanding the best approaches.
—General Thomas Ewing, Official Report, October 20, 1864.[29]

Earlier, in April 1864, Brigadier General L.C. Hunt inspected the conditions at the Knob. He commented on the number of the fort's cannons and the fact that Shepherd Mountain commanded the fortifications but offered no suggestions to remedy the situation. He suggested that barracks be built for the soldiers, who were still for the most part living in tents and shanties. More important than protecting soldiers from exposure, Hunt wanted the horses protected. Hunt accused the regimental officers of "gross negligence," as shelters had not been built for horses, which had been exposed all winter to the elements. His overall concern seems to be that the valley had more men than were needed to combat guerrillas and that if the number of soldiers in the various Missouri state militias were reduced, the horses could be shipped to other theatres of war. He suggested an overall reduction of horses and men of 25 percent.[30]

Planting the Flag on Pilot Knob. From *Frank Leslie's Illustrated Newspaper* September 7, 1861, page 269. *Missouri Department of Natural Resources Fort Davidson Collection, #65-2008-004-0001.*

Engineer Amos Stickney recommended in June that a small fort be placed about sixty feet above the floor of the valley on Rock Mountain. He felt that it would not protect Fort Davidson but would protect the quartermaster's and railroad depots. He commented that water could be obtained by digging down about seventy feet. He didn't rule out higher positions, but those positions would have put the quartermaster's and railroad depots under the gun and not defended from those locations.[31] By August, the building of the supplemental fort had been abandoned.[32] Both Hunt's and Stickney's recommendations, if followed, would not have helped the garrison prepare for what it was about to face.

Just prior to the Battle of Pilot Knob, in the summer of 1864, the local soldiers strengthened the fort, as ordered by General Ewing. As fall approached, and rumors grew stronger of a raid by Rebel forces, the newly recruited 47th Missouri Infantry was put to work:

> *Then details from the 47th Mo. were called for to repair Fort Davidson at Pilot Knob and to dig and build the north rifle pit, extending straight away from the deep wide ditch around the fort, to the brick church house*

Early war fortifications at Pilot Knob. *Missouri Department of Natural Resources Fort Davidson Collection, #65-2001-011-0002 part 2.*

[St. Mary's Catholic Church] *or perhaps a school house, which stood probably 80 or 100 yards north of the fort. This building answered the good purpose of protecting the north end of this rifle pit from Cedar Mt., which stood less than a quarter of a mile north of the fort. The boys cut and hauled logs 12 to 14 inches in diameter and placed them on either side of the rifle pit, so when the dirt was dug and thrown out over these logs, they lay on the brink of the ditch and formed part of the breast works.* [33]

Rifle trenches varied according to the military specifications at time. Generally, they would have been dug to a depth of about two to four feet, with the mounds of dirt on either side of the ditch adding another two to four feet of parapet, thus protecting most of a man's body. These trenches were usually eight to ten feet wide. About sixteen inches above the floor of the pit was a second level, which ran the length of the pit. This served as a bench so that soldiers could rest and also as a step down into the trench. When fighting, the soldiers would aim their muskets through small windows in the sand bags, logs and dirt piled on the sides of the pit and shoot at the enemy. [34]

As refugees and retreating soldiers brought reports of Price's army entering Missouri to Fort Davidson, work continued at a more feverish rate.

Mines atop Pilot Knob after the battle from *Frank Leslie's Illustrated Newspaper* October 22, 1864, page 68. *Missouri Department of Natural Resources Fort Davidson Walt Busch Collection L65-2004-010-0025.*

Besides making a new north rifle pit, soldiers reworked the south rifle pit, which had deteriorated due to the weather since 1863. They also deepened the dry moat around the fort.

During this time, freedmen also worked to improve the fortifications, but probably more interestingly, freed African Americans civilians were trained to man some of the large cannons in the fort. As early as 1863, the local commanders saw that the lack of good cannon crews permanently stationed in Pilot Knob was a problem. The military never did anything about requests to station a crew at Pilot Knob, so apparently one of the post commanders made a decision to train fifty-eight men of company G, 1st Missouri State Militia, and some civilians on the big guns. The civilians serviced at least one thirty-two-pound cannon well during the battle on September 27, until an explosion killed three outright and mortally wounded another.

On September 26, 1864, Rebel forces began to enter the Arcadia Valley and made contact first with soldiers at Russellville road. During the daylight hours, skirmishing continued. After nightfall, the main part of Price's army of at least seven thousand men poured into the valley through Shut-In Gap.[35]

The next day, skirmishing continued during the morning hours as Price and his men pushed the defenders back through Ironton Gap and over Shepherd and Pilot Knob Mountains. About 2:00 p.m. the battle began in earnest. The Rebels, led by General William Cabell—one of the designers of what we know today as the Confederate battle flag—made three charges at the fort and only made it to the moat once. The Rebels were driven back with Ketchum grenades (a relatively new invention that looked like a dart with an oblong ball on the front end of it) and short-fused cannonballs being thrown at them.

As dusk fell, the fort walls still stood unbreached. Now, a decision had to be made. The defenders faced three options. First, surrender. With General Ewing, however, that was not an option. Ewing "believed he [Price] meant to repeat Forrest's game of treachery and deceit at Fort Pillow" and would massacre the black citizens and a few black soldiers under his care.[36] A note sent to Ewing from Confederate colonel Alonzo Slayback "virtually confirmed this fear as Slayback stated that if the fort were taken by assault General Price could not prevent the entire garrison being put to the sword."[37]

The second option was to stay and fight. But ammunition would not last and Price had ten cannons. While the Union artillerymen could defend the fort against a few, their efforts would not hold up against ten blazing cannons. Indeed, the day before Ewing had telegraphed General A.J. Smith that he could "hold the Fort against four or five thousand cavalry & four pieces of artillery, I think."[38] Ewing's use of delaying tactics helped him beat the odds once. Only a gambler would chance another full day of battle.[39] The last option was to break out and fight a retreat. This conclusion was not highly thought of in the ranks:

> *I thought that if we had give old "Pap" Price such an awful thrashing that day, why could we not give him a worse one on the morrow? In fact, if Gen. Ewing and "Dave" Murphy said so, I knew we could! That was Company H's conclusion. Like the girl said, when asked if she didn't want to go to heaven she said, "I'd rather stay where I'm better acquainted." We were then "well acquainted" with old Fort Davidson and his rifle pits; but we were not at all acquainted with evacuation and this cutting-our-way-out business.[40]*

Cutting the way out was the ultimate decision. To do that, Ewing had to make sure that there was no effective force near the escape route. At 9:00 p.m., General Marmaduke wrote to Colonel L.A. MacLean of Price's staff:

Scale model of how Fort Davidson appeared at the time of battle. *Fort Davidson Interpretive Center Exhibit. Photo by author.*

> *My troops are all encamped in the plain & below Ironton with the exception of a force of 4 or 500 men under Col Freeman & Slayback & Capt Jacobs which are stationed on the RR about a mile north of the fort attacked today with instruction to watch & fwd me information immediately of any movement of the enemy or of the arrivals of reinforcements & then they are also informed of Gen'l Shelby's expected arrival and instructed to await any collision with his force.*[41]

Blocked! No way out. Ewing should surrender. To hear some talk, even to this day, about what happened next nears the realm of the miraculous.

Chapter 3

The Death of Fort Davidson

Pilot Knob was never surrendered. We evacuated it and blew up the fort, and the only regret we had was that we could not blow up with it Price and his whole army.
—Colonel Thomas C. Fletcher, Missouri Democrat, *October 14, 1864.*[42]

As the sky reddened and then turned to black, Pilot Knob, although surrounded, was still largely an unoccupied town. Pilot Knob houses and Immanuel Lutheran Church served as Union hospitals, and Major Seymour Carpenter, MD, busied himself bringing in wounded Union men as well as trying to arrange for some of the wounded Confederates. Still, some Confederates roamed freely.

Having decided on retreating, the Potosi-Caledonia road, heading north out of town along the base of Cedar Mountain, seemed Ewing's best option. Slayback was camped between Cedar and Rock Mountains blocking the rail line and within view of the Farmington road. If Potosi could be reached, perhaps Mineral Point, where General A.J. Smith's troops were holding, could be also. It was a chance, and Ewing was willing to take it, but he refused to brazenly roll the dice. Instead, the evacuation was quickly and efficiently prepared. As Ewing wrote:

> *The chief danger was, that the preparations for the retreat might be observed, and the garrison cut to pieces or captured, in the confusion incident to the exit. The works of the Iron Company at the north base of Pilot Knob had been fired by the enemy, and the immense pile of*

The Ironton House, the main area hospital during the war, circa 1880. *Courtesy of Jack Mayes.*

charcoal [according to Colonel Fletcher, a pile as large as the Lindell Hotel in St. Louis[43]] *glowed and flamed all night, making the valley as light as noonday. Moreover, I learned Col. Slayback's command held the Mineral Point road just north of the town, leaving the Potosi road the only exit not certainly in the possession of the enemy. But, with all its dangers, the policy of retreat was clearly best; and preparations for it began at midnight. I had Colonel Fletcher arrange for having the magazine, (which was large and filled with every variety of ammunition) blown up in two hours after we left, or as soon as our exit should be discovered by the enemy. We took possession of the town and valley, and drove thence all straggling rebels.*[44]

Most people, including the escaping Union soldiers, found it amazing that they slipped out under the noses of Slayback and Colonel Archibald Dobbins's troops, who were camped west of the Potosi-Caledonia road (basically modern-day Highway 21). However, the assumption that most of Dobbin's camp was within a few hundred feet of the Potosi road is wrong.

As Ewing commented above, he sent in scouts to clear the town and the road—quietly, discretely, before the soldiers marched out of the fort. This

Scarred Iron County Courthouse, probably in the fall of 1864, after the Union reoccupied the Arcadia Valley. *Courtesy of Jack Mayes.*

would have cleared the area around the road, which Dobbins's main force was simply not protecting. While they may have been able to see it during the day, it was barely visible at night from their camp.

Although strong archaeological evidence has not determined the precise location of Dobbins's camp, the speculation as to where it was is simple enough. At the end of the day of battle, with the Union still holding the fort, the soldiers commanded a large field of fire with muskets and cannons. Only a Rebel with a death wish would light a campfire a few hundred yards from the fort on the plain or mountainsides. Any attempt to camp near the fort all night invited any one of a thousand Union soldiers to pop off a couple rounds at the light. No, the only Rebels within small arms range were the wounded, writhing in pain on the field.[45]

With the way clear, Ewing's force needed to silently make its preparations to leave. Officers issued whispered commands throughout the fort. "Gather ammunition! 100 Rounds!" "Secure rations!" "Cannon crews…Spike your guns!" "Pile the dead atop the powder magazine!" "Gather up the wounded and get them to Dr. Carpenter!" "Sorry, Captain Jim, they'll hang you for sure if you're seen! But, we'll get you to a hospital when we leave."[46] "I need you, you and you! Put hay on the drawbridge to deaden the sound of the horses and wagons! Lay tents across it, too!" "Sneak out of the fort and bring in some horse!"[47] "Leave those 2 inch guns behind, they're useless. And the mortars, too! Take the others! Wrap their wheels in canvas with leather strips so they don't make any noise!" "Put those caissons against the wall of the magazine, let them burn as well!" Quietly and quickly, soldiers performed their tasks; what started out as mass confusion by the soldiers coalesced into an organized, efficient and unified team.

Sometime between midnight and 1:30 a.m. on the twenty-eighth, depending on whose story you're reading, the command formed up. General Ewing had a detachment of his veteran 14th Iowa, commanded by Captain William Campbell, lead the way. Colonel Fletcher assigned one hundred veterans in command by First Lieutenant James McMurtry as the advance of his infantry. They marched across the drawbridge and down into the north rifle pit. After the infantry came the artillery, and finally the cavalry, with another detachment of the 14th Iowa bringing up the rear. Ewing had nearly two hundred civilians with him as he left. Many of them were not happy about how they were treated by Ewing and his command; the Germans particularly complained later:

> *The fort was to be evacuated by the military on the 27th after midnight according to the arrangements made by General Ewing. The citizens remained unconsidered and on request to General Ewing made by Mr. Marion as to what advice he would give the citizens, the general answered him with "Let them lay down their arms and surrender." Instead, the citizens preferred to follow the military.*[48]

General Thomas Ewing. *Digital Photo Collection, Library of Congress. Call no. LC-DIG-cwpbh-00680.*

As they left the fort's rifle pit, they formed up on the shadowy west side of St. Mary's church out of the light being thrown by the burning charcoal pile. They moved up the Potosi road, and as they passed Immanuel Lutheran Church, the soldiers left the stretcher carrying James "Captain Jim" Farrar there. They continued moving silently, watching the campfires of Dobbins's troops burning in hues of orange on the plain. The large, looming shadows of Rebels keeping warm against the flames made them seem much closer than they truly were.

Prior to leaving the fort, during the war council to determine what should be done, Ewing decided to blow up the fort. He commanded Captain H.B. Milks to lead the team that was to be left behind. As Ewing's column left the fort, Captain Milks reports:

> *Lieutenant Copp, Sergt. W.H. Moore, of my company, and I went down into the powder magazine, knocked open powder kegs and made a pile of powder as large as a hay-cock in the center of the magazine. The room was forty feet long, twelve feet high, and twelve feet wide. A section through the center was filled from bottom to top with kegs of powder and fixed ammunition. No fuse being at hand, a trail was laid from the pile of powder out over the drawbridge.*[49]

After these preparations were made, the demolition team found five soldiers still sleeping, exhausted from all the fighting. They awoke after being shaken and kicked back into consciousness. As they moved around the fort looking for soldiers left behind, the team looked at the fifteen bodies piled up near the magazine.[50] Soon the dead would be buried "with honors."

Now, about twenty-five men waited until 3:00 a.m., when Sergeant Moore reported that the magazine had been fired.[51] Moore mounted his horses and, together with the others, trotted out of the fort. Setting spurs to their mounts, they got about seventy-five yards when a blinding light flashing continually crossed the sky, followed by a large explosion and then many smaller ones. Twenty thousand pounds of black powder had flashed, throwing timbers, lead shot and dead bodies high into the air. The concussion of the explosion ripped through fabric and tore limbs off bodies. The explosion propelled the garrison

General Sterling Price. *Digital Photo Collection, Library of Congress. Call no. LC-DIG-cwpd-07527.*

flagpole holding Old Glory, left behind to deceive the Confederates into believing that the command was still in the fort, into the air as a fireball surrounded it. The deafening sound could be heard for twenty miles—some say thirty. Ewing's command heard it and quickened their pace.

Private Amos Thomas Long, who was not found in the fort by Milks's demolition team, awoke to the violent pressure changes and sound of the explosion and was immediately buried alive under a pile of dirt. Along with another civilian who slept through the evacuation, he dug his way out; after dressing up and serving a few days in the Rebel army, he eventually made it back to his company.[52] One ridiculous anecdotal story claims that an African American was asleep atop the magazine, which blew him up into the air. Landing in an all-out run, he hurried back to Ironton. But that was just an old children's bedtime story as outdated today as Uncle Remus's.[53] The flag fell to the ground. The groggy Rebels sat straight up, decided that the powder magazine inside Fort Davidson had exploded, killing all the Union soldiers, and went back to sleep.

Captain David Corder, injured during the attack on Pilot Knob and later taken to Alton Prison. *Missouri Department of Natural Resources Fort Davidson Collection, #65-2007-002-0001.*

The next morning, General Sterling Price and his army discovered that the enemy had slipped out of the fort. Some citizens who had sat atop the nearby mountains watching the battle, and the women and children who had sheltered inside the local beer cave at Ironton Gap, came out onto the battlefield to look for men they knew. Mrs. Herman "Hattie" Davis walked the field and found her country's tattered, scarred flag laying on the ground. Concealing it, she took it home and kept it for the rest of her life.[54] Christian Hollatz was found and later buried in Pilot Knob Cemetery, but some people were never found.[55]

Price sent one-third of his soldiers chasing after the escaping Union soldiers under

General Thomas Ewing through the St. Francois mountains and Ozark hills. Some of the Rebels remained behind to gather supplies in the nearby towns and fort, which according to Captain T.J. Mackey, CSA engineers, amounted to the following:

> [The fort's] *armament, consisting of 4 32-pounder guns, 4 24-pounder howitzers on garrison carriages, 4 6-inch Coehorn mortars, 4 steel 2-pounder skirmish guns, together with many hundred rounds of fixed ammunition for these guns; a large amount of ammunition for small-arms, and about eight or ten days' rations for 1,000 men; some 100 or 200 blankets; also the foundry, furnaces, and all the work-shops of the Pilot Knob Iron Company…and 2,000 pounds of coffee.*[56]

While many gathered supplies, others worked inside the hospitals and buried the dead in the rifle pits of the fort. An ambulance escort, led by Colonel James Rains, took some of the walking wounded south, back to Arkansas.[57] How many died and were wounded is a good question, but claims of about 300 to 400 Rebel dead and 900 to 1,200 wounded are not impossible. Ewing lost 14 killed, 14 mortally wounded, 44 wounded, 9 minorly wounded and 1 missing in two days of battle. He reported the Union losses at about 200 killed, wounded and missing over the entire engagement and retreat.[58]

On October 13, units of the 10th Kansas Infantry, commanded by Major H.H. Williams, entered the Arcadia Valley to find only a skeleton crew of Rebel hospital orderlies and doctors caring for their wounded.[59] Several were still dying of injuries each day. Many had recovered enough to be transported, first to the Gratiot Street prison in St. Louis and then to Rock Island or Alton prisons. The dead who hadn't been buried in the south rifle pit still lay out on the hillsides surrounding the burned, scarred fort. First Sergeant James A. Smith, Company D, 10th Kansas Veteran Volunteers, reported:

> [We] *left St. Louis for Pilot Knob, having in charge 200 prisoners to be used in repairing the Fort and remounting the heavy guns that had been thrown down by the force of the explosion of the magazine which was blown up by a detail left behind by General Ewing. The Kansas troops arrived at Pilot Knob on the 24th (of October) and finding so many dead producing a stifling odor, began the internment of the putrefying bodies at once. Details were sent out under non-commissioned officers using the*

Ruins of the fort from *Every Saturday* magazine December 9, 1871. *Missouri Department of Natural Resources Fort Davidson Collection, #65-2007-005-0001.*

prisoners for fatigue duty. A strict search was made up and down the Valley, upon the slopes of Pilot Knob and Shepherd's Mountains and about 125 Confederates were buried. All were interred where they were found as it was impossible to remove them. Graves were dug beside the bodies which were pushed into their last resting places with spades and covered up with nothing to mark the place. Often, by watching dogs going and coming from the brush covering the sides of the mountains, bodies would be found. One or two more found on the summit of Shepherd's Mountain where a Confederate battery had been stationed…It was currently reported by our men that the body of a woman was found among the Confederate dead having been killed in the assault on the Union fort. I am unable to vouch for the correctness of this report but it was generally regarded as a fact at the time we were in Pilot Knob.[60]

Chapter 4

Reconstructed...from the Ashes

The war was not yet over. After bridges were repaired, Pilot Knob still needed to serve the Union cause. More iron needed producing. In mid-October, the Arcadia Valley was garrisoned once again by Union soldiers, and work crews began repairing the damage. On October 17, 1864, General Ewing requested that the St. Louis Arsenal send ammunition for the four thirty-two-pounders and three twenty-four-pound howitzers that Price's army was forced to leave behind.[61] While some repairs could be made rapidly, many languished, as rounding up guerrillas and reclaiming the countryside was militarily more important in the wake of Price's raid.

By December 1864, Lieutenant Colonel David Murphy, who was serving as inspector for the District of St. Louis, reported:

> *Since the invasion by Price in October the post of Pilot Knob presents rather a dilapidated appearance. The quartermaster's department, in charge of Captain Dyer, is not characterized by that high state of efficiency for which it has been mentioned in previous reports. Captain Dyer has since been relieved (by reason of sickness); his place is filled by Lieutenant White, regimental quartermaster, Fiftieth Infantry Missouri Volunteers. It is to be hoped that the public buildings necessary to shelter the public animals will be brought to a state of completion before the return of spring. The subsistence department, in charge of Captain May, commissary of subsistence, performs its functions in the usual creditable manner. Supplies are on hand sufficient for two months. The hospital, in charge of Dr.*

T.W. Johnson, acting assistant surgeon, is in an excellent condition. There are eighty-two patients, twenty-four of whom are Confederate (wounded) soldiers. Doctor Johnson preserves the utmost order and compliance on the part of occupants, attendants, &c., with usual regulations governing military hospitals. The refugee department, in charge of Rev. L.T. McNeiley, chaplain Third Cavalry Missouri State Militia, exhibits a marked improvement in the management of affairs. The chaplain was reported by my predecessor as having given orders for 4,500 rations in four days. This report, I believe, did the chaplain injustice, as it implied that to be the average number of rations issued. The chaplain explains by saying that whilst the road was severed, and communication destroyed with Saint Louis, that great difficulty occurred in procuring rations. Captain Huiskamp visited the post just as the first supply was received, consequently a great rush was made by the starving refugees on the commissary department; hence the basis for the report. The number of rations issued from December 1 to December 24, 1864, was 6,584. This includes issues to sick in refugee hospital and contrabands.[62]

As spring progressed, Sherman started off for South Carolina. Then came April, and suddenly the war was over. The war department immediately discharged soldiers (all but members of the United States Colored Troops, who usually had to serve out their whole term of service), Rebel officers and soldiers were pardoned and civilian life began to return to normal. Plans prepared by Captain William Hoelcke to strengthen Fort Davidson, including the placing of bomb-proofs over and surrounding each cannon, were forgotten by all but the designer.[63]

When the military departed, the old fort field was taken over again by the mining company. Over the years, it served as a corral for mules and oxen, while the iron company used the field around it to dump crushed rock after having the ores extracted. The abuse of the land did not go on forever. Many people, particularly the officers of the Iron Mountain Railroad, recognized the restful qualities of the Arcadia Valley and began touting it as a day excursion site from St. Louis. Indeed, even German magazines advertised the serenity of the valley, promoting that great Victorian pastime, the picnic:

Pilot Knob, as well as the Iron Mountains in general, are easy to get to from St. Louis. Since the Knob itself offers really marvelous places, areas with rough and fissures, frequently in the summer excursions and picnic parties come there from St. Louis. Here they can find an abundance of romantic, beautiful sites with plenty of shade, pure fresh air, and magnificent views. One has a surprisingly excellent view especially from the peak of the Knob and it is indeed worth the effort in spite of the not insignificant exertion to climb to its top.[64]

By 1882, eighteen years after the Battle of Pilot Knob, an executive committee was formed by local survivors of the battle to have a celebration at the old fort. While enthusiasm was high, the organizers called for annual meetings. Hoping for a larger turnout, the next meeting was to be held in a year's time at the unveiling of the monument that members of the 21st Illinois Infantry were erecting to honor U.S. Grant. Unfortunately, that event did not take place until 1886.

That September, as plans for the anniversary of the battle and the dedication of the Grant monument began going forward, some railroads failed to give the needed discounts for the veterans to travel cheaply. At the last minute (September 23), the battle celebration was called off. The Grant monument in Emerson Park (now the churchyard at Ste. Marie du Lac Roman Catholic Church) was dedicated, and a much more subdued celebration occurred.

That seemingly would have been the death knell of any organization of battle survivors or of preserving the fort were it not for the interest of a few men—mainly Dr. Cyrus A. Peterson, Henry C. Wilkinson and Thomas Ewing, son of the general.

Chapter 5

Tenting on the Old Campground

As the horrors of war receded in memories and the soldiers aged, people began to wax nostalgic about their accomplishments. This had started already during the war, but the 1880s saw new vigor and impetus to memorialize the war. The boys in blue had, as early as 1865, organized themselves into the Grand Army of the Republic (GAR), with the principal aim of the organization being employment for veterans. One of the first commanders of the Missouri GAR was Colonel David Murphy, who was in charge of the artillery at Pilot Knob.[65] By the 1868 campaigns, the national organization became embroiled in politics, and membership rapidly fell. However, the mid-1880s saw the group revitalize, reorganize and reemerge on the national scene. GAR posts began springing up all over the country in almost every town.

The 1880s saw the end of Radical Reconstruction in the South and the resurrection of Confederate political power as well. Former Confederates began holding government jobs, which didn't suit many boys in blue who also would have liked those jobs. In Missouri, former Confederate general John S. Marmaduke became the governor, and many other Confederates returned to political power. To promote their own political agenda, GAR members waved the "bloody banner" to fight for compensation for those who remained true to the flag. The desire by veterans to be compensated for their service swelled the ranks of the GAR. By the end of the decade, Missouri had more than four hundred posts after beginning the 1880s with barely two hundred.[66] The organization attempted to stay away from party politics, adjusting its goals to work for veterans' benefits, memorialize its honored dead and promote patriotism in the great United States and comradery amongst the old veterans.

Posts were named for soldiers, battles, military objects or duty. Farmington Post 215 was named the Picket Post. The Ironton Post 346 was the Iron Post. Several Missouri posts took the names of soldiers who fought in the Battle of Pilot Knob or in the events leading up to it, such as Lieutenant Erich Pape Post 184 (Zalma), Major James Wilson Post 20 (Louisiana), Colonel Amos W. Maupin Post 586 (Old Soldier's Home, St. James) and Lieutenant William Brawner Post 394 (Patton). Probably Poplar Bluff's veterans named the Captain Hendricks Post 590 after a Pilot Knob veteran, John W. Hendricks. Pilot Knob did not have a post until after 1900. Its post, 579, was named in honor of U.S. Grant.

Besides gathering for Memorial Day observances or when veterans passed away, these camps often had campfires—a time in the evening after the day's business when the old veterans gathered around the fire, told stories and sung the songs of old. General W.T. Sherman, a member of the Ransom Post in St. Louis, considered this the best part of the organization.[67] In Pilot Knob, the GAR would gather and hold its campfires inside Fort Davidson. Many of the dances and formal meetings also took place at the old Union church, which was located only two hundred yards east of the fort.[68]

Confederate veterans were also getting very active during this time. Immediately after the war, the boys in gray were banned from gathering in many places and could not hold public events. This led to their wives and daughters memorializing battles and the dead and becoming deeply engaged in creating the myth of the Lost Cause. The United Daughters of the Confederacy (UDC) outshone all other organizations in making sure through monuments and historic markers that the "Southern truth" to history was proclaimed throughout the land.[69] By the end of Reconstruction, southern men could once again openly wear the gray and organize themselves. The chief organization was the United Confederate Veterans (UCV).

The UCV never achieved as many posts as the GAR; still, it was popular in Missouri. Seventy-seven posts existed by 1900. Of these, many honored officers who served in Price's raid. Major General Sterling Price and Major General John S. Marmaduke each had three camps named after them, while General J.O. Shelby had two and General John B. Clark Jr. had one honoring him. Colonels David Shanks, Thomas R. Freeman, Solomon G. Kitchen, William L. Jeffers and Captain Samuel S. Harris each had a camp also honoring them. The camp at the State Home for Confederate Veterans at Higginsville

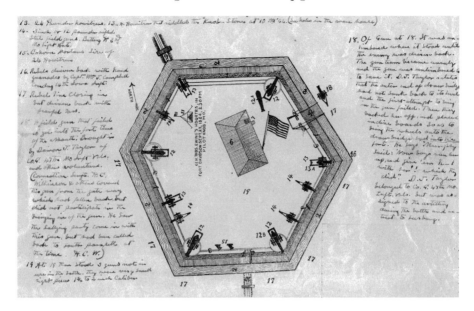

Diagram of fort with Sergeant H.C. Wilkinson's notes on them. See Appendix 2 for text. *Missouri Department of Natural Resources Fort Davidson Collection, #65-1998-001-0001.*

View of the Armored Plan, part 2, with Wilkinson's notes. See Appendix 2 for text. *Missouri Department of Natural Resources Fort Davidson Collection, #65-1998-001-0001.*

was named after Colonel John N. Edwards of Shelby's brigade. The closest posts to the Arcadia Valley were the Crow Camp 712 at Farmington and the Colonel Lowe Camp 805 at Fredericktown.[70] Groups like the GAR, UDC and UCV helped keep the memories of the war alive and taught the varied histories of the war to the young. As more and more organizations formed to memorialize the war, a drive began with Dr. Cyrus Peterson to preserve the memory of the Battle of Pilot Knob and the battlefield.

Dr. Peterson was the son of Corporal Daniel Peterson, Company H, 3rd Missouri State Militia Cavalry, who fought at Pilot Knob. At age twenty,

Two photos with battle positions marked on them from between 1900 and 1910. See Appendix 2 for text. *Missouri Department of Natural Resources Fort Davidson Collection, #65-1998-001-0001.*

Text with Sergeant Wilkinson's notes. See Appendix 2 for text. *Missouri Department of Natural Resources Fort Davidson Collection, #65-1998-001-0001.*

in 1869, Cyrus ambushed and almost killed the noted bushwhacker Sam Hildebrand. He held a deep-seated bitterness toward Rebels and bushwhackers because his "only brother was sacrificed for the Union cause and my father came out of the Union army a broken down man in 1865."[71]

His father died in 1884, and Peterson set out on the task to preserve his memory by protecting the battlefield and documenting the battle that had helped shatter the health of his father.[72]

By the turn of the twentieth century, Dr. Peterson began corresponding with several people and collecting information about the battle. One very prolific correspondent was former sergeant Henry C. Wilkinson, Company H, 47th Missouri Infantry. Although Wilkinson had seen much service in local units (Captain Powers's Independent Cavalry and the 68th Enrolled Missouri Militia, also known as the Haw Eaters), he also felt that his greatest service had come during what he called "the Great Little Battle" and the subsequent retreat.[73] Wilkinson began acting as Peterson's investigator, interviewing old comrades, drawing maps of the battlefield and providing any information he could, while Peterson researched information on the units in the Missouri adjutant general's office. Together, by 1914, their work resulted in the publication of *Pilot Knob: Thermopylae of the West*, which Peterson coauthored with Joseph M. Hanson. It also resulted in a massive collection of papers now located in the archives of the Missouri Historical Society.

The contacts made by these men with old comrades and friends for this project created the desire to meet on the battlefield. So, in 1903, calls went out to hold a reunion the next year on the anniversary of the battle. They contacted the sons of General Ewing, Thomas and William, both of whom agreed to come to the celebration. Thomas had worked with his father in patent law until his father's accidental death. After that, he became a well-respected patent lawyer in his own right. While his father had been a state supreme court judge and had performed other services for his country during his life, his greatest military feat occurred at Pilot Knob and in the subsequent retreat. Thomas, ultimately, became the man burdened with the responsibility to see that the desires of all these old veterans came to fruition.

Chapter 6

Where the Cannons Use to Roar

O n September 27, 1904, the first general meeting of the Pilot Knob Memorial Association took place on the old battlefield. To the survivors gathered, the greatness of the battle resounded in the hyperbole, metaphors and similes they created for it: "Thermopylae of the West," "Missouri's Alamo," "like Marathon" and more. Likenesses to each of those battles can be drawn, and the Union men gathered at these reunions wanted their battle memorialized similarly. Their first reunion since 1882 was a huge success and as such continued for several years until 1910, when the event was cancelled at the last minute because special rates could not be obtained for transportation from the railroads. In 1911, the railroads again gave discounted rates, and the celebration went off as planned. During this time, three printed editions of the proceedings are known to have been made: 1904, 1905 and 1906. The local newspapers printed parts of other proceedings for all, it seems, but the 1909 celebration.

There are no records of events in 1912 or '13, and by the time of the fiftieth anniversary of the battle in 1914, Thomas Ewing and his daughter were seemingly the only people interested in having a celebration. The days of the Pilot Knob Memorial Association had ended. Fortunately, the members accomplished most of what they set out to do.

The association decided by 1905 to buy the fort and some of the battlefield. This might have been a problem prior to then, because the Big Muddy Coal & Iron Company owned the land. Unfortunately for the mining company, the good veins of iron were finally thinning out. As Big

Muddy slowed its operations, it began divesting itself of its local assets, which resulted in the selling of most of its landholdings in the area to the South Hungarian Colonization & Land Company for $30,000.[74] Now, with the colonization company wanting to sell off land in small lots, the time was right to acquire the fort property. The association had been created at the right time, and it generated enough interest that on December 11, 1905, 19.24 acres containing Fort Davidson were purchased in the names of Cyrus Peterson, Thomas Ewing Jr. and a man who was the seventh vice-president of the 1904 World's Fair, August Gehner.[75] The price was $1,443.

After the purchase of the land, the veterans began pushing to make it a national battlefield. To do this, a bill was presented in Congress, but it never passed.[76] While Pilot Knob battlefield was the first in the state to be protected by an organization, Wilson's Creek was also being promoted by old Missouri veterans. In the end, the Wilson's Creek lobby succeeded in obtaining national battlefield status for that land.

Aside from the battlefield purchase, the Pilot Knob Memorial Association held reunions and campfires on this land and began planning improvements. At reunions, there were requests for people to position themselves on the field where they were the day of battle so that markers could eventually be placed. The group also wanted a memorial monument placed in the center of the old fort. The association considered seeking the advice of the United Daughters of the Confederacy in the creation of a monument. Whether it did or not is unknown, but generating Confederate organizations' interest in this battle was difficult at best.

There were several problems with trying to involve Confederate organizations in this effort. First, while the Confederates could claim a "victory" by the fact that they held the field at the end of the day, the deaths of so many soldiers and escape of the Federal army made it a strategic disaster. While General Sterling Price did not have the organized detractors that General Longstreet had in the aftermath of the war, most former Missouri Rebels considered his 1864 raid a messy affair at best. Memorializing a failed campaign was the last thing that former Rebels would want to do.[77] However, to look at Price's raid as a total disaster is a mistake.

The initial goals of Sterling Price were to raid supplies, obtain manpower and, if possible, seize supply depots in St. Louis and Jefferson City. That was all that was expected of him.[78] He personally wanted to try to stay long enough in the state to influence the state and national elections.[79] Many Missouri Confederate politicians also held that high hope. Price achieved the first two results but failed in the others. Indeed, his influence on the election

Survivors at the 1905 reunion. See Appendix 2 for text. *Missouri Department of Natural Resources Fort Davidson Collection, #65-1998-001-0001.*

helped promote Colonel Thomas Fletcher (who was second in command of Union soldiers at Pilot Knob) as the hero and favorite gubernatorial candidate of Missourians. This resulted in Fletcher freeing Missouri's slaves in January 1865.

Most stop their analysis of Price's raid at this point; because of that, the boys in gray and their sons and daughters want to forget the raid. This is a disservice to all of the Confederate soldiers who died or were wounded at Pilot Knob, Big Blue, Westport, Mine Creek and other battles. It was very successful in pulling troops away from General Thomas at Nashville and General Canby at Mobile. Sherman had to wait two months longer than he wanted to start his march to the sea because support troops had to go to or stay in Missouri. The Union authorities had to activate large numbers of civilians into service, disrupting the economy. In fact, several historians point to the fact that if the Mobile operations were allowed to begin on time, the war would have been shortened by as much as four months. So Price's raid was a disruptive success on a very large scale.

The problem, as these researchers see it, lies in the fact that Hood in Tennessee, Lee in Virginia and Confederate forces in Arkansas and Georgia did not take immediate action. If they had, Nashville might have fallen and Sherman might have had to fight his way back from Atlanta. During this time, only Generals Forrest and Early seemed to periodically be on

Another photo of the survivors. *Missouri Department of Natural Resources Fort Davidson Collection.*

the offensive. The failure of the Confederate government to recognize the boon Price's raid was giving them and coordinating efforts in all theatres of actions truly helped influence the elections and easily gave President Lincoln a second term.[80]

Another reason the Confederate survivors of the battle did not flock to join the organization was that Union survivors, led by Dr. Peterson and Colonel Murphy, controlled it. Both were ardent Union men. Peterson, in particular, wanted to memorialize the Federal soldiers at the battle as great defenders and saviors of Missouri. For that reason, when writing his book he fails to correspond with or gather much information from Rebel sources (Generals William Cabell and James Fagan were still alive and could have added some perspective to the battle). This was unfortunate for the organization and eliminated much of the support the organization could have had, especially since all the soldiers were aging.

August Gehner died within three years of the land being obtained. Cyrus Peterson was also aging and suffering ill health.[81] By 1914, the fiftieth anniversary of the battle, Iron Post 346 had only three men in it, and Grant Post 579, which mustered the required number of men to obtain an official charter about 1904, failed to maintain that number within a few short years. With Congress failing to recognize the site as a national battlefield and the memorial association's members dying, the preservation of the field fell to the general's son.

Thomas Ewing lived in Yonkers, New York, but regularly worked in Washington, D.C. Many difficulties were present for him that hindered him in protecting this land. Born in 1862, he was almost fifty years old when he obligated himself to try to do something to preserve this battlefield. He obtained Cyrus Peterson's share of the land in 1909 and that of the August Gehner's family in 1910.[82] In 1913, to make it more attractive as a potential park to a government agency, he bought 3.03 acres adjacent to it.[83] At the time of the fiftieth anniversary of the battle, he returned to Ironton in the hope that the city would accept the land for free as long as they promised to maintain it as a memorial park. He was unsuccessful in this endeavor.

During the next twenty years, he tried to give the land to several different government agencies. All turned him down. In 1934, the Missouri Highway Commission bought 0.3 acres from him so that it could run Highway 21 (now Highway 221 or South McCune Street) on the west side of the fort.[84] Thomas Ewing was now in his seventies, and time was running out. He touted the land again to government agencies and was finally successful in giving it to the U.S. Forest Service, with a provision:

> *The grantors herein reserve unto themselves, their heirs and assigns, the right to commemorate the history of Fort Davidson, which is located upon said land, by the erection of a monument suitable to themselves and by providing for the perpetual maintenance of same. In the event of the erection of any such monument, the same to be erected and completed within a period of twenty (20) years from the date hereof, and is to be erected on that portion of Lots Fifty-five (55) and Sixty-four (64), which is known as Fort Davidson, or the land lying between Fort Davidson and Missouri State Highway Number Twenty-One (21).*[85]

The U.S. Forest Service saw the Fort Davidson Recreational Area, as they called it, as something to maintain with minimal work being done to protect it. Except for a sign, interpretation was nonexistent. The Forest Service had no problem with a monument being installed on the earthworks as long as it did not have to pay for it or its maintenance. This is understandable as the Forest Service, especially in the '40s and '50s, was an agency working with timber management; recreation was secondary, and historic interpretation wasn't even on the radar screen. So, all interpretation was left to others.

In May 1941, E.W. Woods, district ranger of the Clark National Forest stationed at Fredericktown, wrote a short report about Fort Davidson reporting conversations he had with two unnamed men about the battle and

Sergeant H.C. Wilkinson (foreground, left) and Private Azariah Martin (foreground, right) with 4th U.S. Cavarly soldiers at a reunion. *Missouri Department of Natural Resources Fort Davidson Collection, #65-1998-001-0002.*

the fort. Although the men claim to have been witnesses to the battle as boys, some of the facts they provided were amusing. What is interesting about the report is the statement that the "draw bridge [entrance] on the east side… can still be seen."[86]

The drawbridge area is slightly visible in several turn-of-the-century photographs, but by the time the U.S. Forest Service owned the land, it had been gone for many years. The new entrance was in place as early as the 1900s with a little wood bridge over the parapet and fence to allow people access to the fort. Near the new entrance, the Missouri Highway Commission posted a painted wooden sign:

> *FORT DAVIDSON*
> *Scene of the Battle of Pilot Knob Sept. 26 and 27, 1864. This fort thrown up and occupied by the Federal Forces under General Ewing repulsed the attack of the Confederate Army under General Price who occupied Shepherd Mountain on the South following renewed attacks by*

*augmented southern forces General Ewing on the night of Sept. 27 1864
blew up the magazine and retreated following Route 21 to Caledonia thence
over the Belgrade Road to Leasburg.*
—*Missouri State Highway Commission*—[87]

That sign was very similar to the one put up in the 1920s by the Arcadia Valley Commercial Club.[88] It is amusing in itself. While it says that "General Ewing" fought General Price, it failed to say which General Ewing. Many Missouri history books at the turn of the century said that it was Hugh Ewing, Tom's brother, a mistake that goes back to Horace Greeley's history of the war.[89] So, interpretation was very open to, well, interpretation.

Until 1953, that was the only interpretation of the battle and fort. Then the highway commission joined with the State Historical Society of Missouri and placed a historical marker and a rest stop to the north of the earthworks. After that marker went up, two cannons were placed nearby and multiflora rose was planted on the fort to protect the walls.

In the early 1960s, interest grew as the country celebrated the centennial of the Civil War. On the hundredth anniversary of the battle, large crowds gathered to participate in a commemoration ceremony. Modern army howitzer blasts echoed through the valley, harkening back to the thirty-two-pounders one hundred years before. The Missouri State Park Board took note of the public interest in the Civil War and entered into an agreement with the U.S. Forest Service to manage the fort as a historic site in 1969. In 1970, Fort Davidson achieved a place on the National Register of Historic Places (#70000332). The management agreement between the Forest Service and Missouri Division of State Parks lasted for the next eighteen years until 1987, when the Missouri Department of Natural Resources acquired the land of what was now the Fort Davidson State Historic Site. The monument that so many sought for so long to create was finally born.[90]

Chapter 7

Retelling the Battle

The Iron County Register, *1882*

From the Iron County Register, *Ironton, Missouri, Thursday, September 7, 1882, page 4, columns two and three.*

A MEMORABLE BATTLE

———

The Story of the Engagement at
Pilot Knob Retold.

———

M any who participated in the Battle of Pilot Knob, fought on September 26–27, 1864, will this year take passage for the old battleground, and, in wine and song, celebrate the eighteenth anniversary of the event which will ever be part and parcel of Missouri's history. Many stories have been told of the fight at Pilot Knob, and more than one claimed that it was a grand victory for the Confederates, for at the end of the second day the Federals withdrew from their position. Some have seen fit to call the retreat a route, but it was the very wisest move the Federals could make, as they had finished the task cut out for them, obeyed all orders and did all they had to do boldly and well. That their movements satisfied those in authority was proven a few days later when Gen. Rosecrans, with headquarters at St. Louis, issued the following order:

Headquarters, Department of the Missouri,
St. Louis, Mo., October 6, 1864.
—General Order, No. 189.—With pride and pleasure the commanding
General notices the gallant conduct of Brigadier-General Thomas Ewing,
Jr., and his command, in the defense of Pilot Knob, and in the subsequent
retreat to Rolla. With scarcely 1,000 effective men they repulsed the attacks
of Price's invading army, and successfully retreated with their battery
a distance of 100 miles in the face of a pursuing and assailling [sic]
cavalry force of five times their number. Such conduct deserves imitation,
particularly when contrasted with the cowardly conduct of the troops at
Osage Bridge. The General commanding presents his hearty thanks and
congratulations to the commanding officers of troops and the staff officers.
Under such commanders Federal troops should always march to victory.

By command of Maj.-Gen. Rosecrans.
FRANK ENO, A.A.G.

THE STORY OF THE BATTLE

Last night a veteran who took part in the fight and whose memory covers every material point, told the story of the battle in corroboration of the statement made by Rosecrans, and the bravery of those who took part in the engagement. The Confederates had three divisions, or 12,000 men in arms, and these were commanded by Gen. Price and Major-Generals Cabell, Fagan and Marmaduke. The Federals had one company of infantry of the Missouri State militia, numbering 60 men; one company of the 2d Missouri volunteer artillery; two companies of the 14th Iowa volunteers; two companies of the 3d regiment M.S.M.; one company of the 2d cavalry M.SM., all numbering about forty to the company; five companies of the 47th Regiment, Missouri Volunteer Infantry, sixty men to the company; one company of the 50th Missouri Volunteers, and some few citizens. All told the Federals numbered less than 1,000 to their opponents [*sic*] 12,000. The Federals camped in the valley at the foot of Pilot Knob and near the fort erected there. Gen. Ewing was in command. Col. Thos. Fletcher commanded the 47th Regiment; Maj. Jas. Wilson, the 3d Cavalry; First-Lieutenant David Murphy, the 50th Missouri; Capt. W.J. Campbell, the 14th Iowa; Capt. W.C. Montgomery, one company of the 2d Missouri Artillery; Capt. A.M. Wright, the 2d Cavalry M.S.M., the Lieut. John Fesler, the 1st Infantry M.S.M., acting as heavy artillery. The cavalry, commanded by Capt. [Major] Wilson, took their position at the foot of the Knob. Capt. Campbell's command was located across Shepherd Mountain, with instructions to retire before any force that the outset appeared too heavy for them. The 47th Regiment and one company of the 50th Missouri were stationed in the ditch connecting to the fort with the town of Pilot Knob, while the 1st Regiment of the Missouri State Militia manned the 32 and 24-pound garrison guns. The 2d Missouri artillery also took up their station within the fort, mounting their four guns on a temporary platform. Two additional pieces of artillery were placed in charge of Lieutenant Smiley. These were on the extreme flank of the Infantry in the ditch at the edge of

The Town of Pilot Knob

For the Confederates, Shelby was sent around by way of Farmington with instructions to hold the road at Potosi and from that point to St. Louis. Cabell and Fagan were placed in charge of the assaulting columns. Marmaduke held Shepherd Mountain with his artillery and supporting forces. Price stationed himself at Arcadia, two miles from the battle ground. There had been skirmishing from the morning of September 26 until night, in the vicinity of Shut-In Gap, below Arcadia. At night Ewing resolved to make a stand and thus compel Price to develop his entire force. The fort was placed in condition to receive four light pieces. These were erected on platforms. On the morning of the 27th the troops were in position and the battle was commenced by Marmaduke's division taking possession of Shepherd Mountain and driving before it the two companies of the 14th Iowa who returned by the mountain slope and centered [reentered] the fort by means of the ditch connecting it with the foot of the mountain. Late in the morning Marmaduke succeeded in planting four guns on the eastern slope of the mountain, directly opposite the fort. Lieut. Murphy saw this move, but refused to open fire, desiring to give the Confederate General all the time he needed in which to plant his guns. Gen. Ewing, on the other hand, kept insisting that they should open on Marmaduke with the garrison guns, but not a shot was fired until the Confederate force sent a ball in the Federal camp. This was the opening signal. Lieut. Murphy jumped upon the platform and training the 32-pounder gave orders to fire, which were promptly obeyed. The shot struck on the slope and disabled one of Marmaduke's guns. This satisfied the Confederates for the first time that there was to be a fight, and rejoiced at the prospect, they sent up a cheer. From that moment every gun in the fort was called into play. There was a duel of artillery that lasted half an hour, at the expiration of which time Marmaduke was obliged to withdraw his battery out of range of the fire from the fort. As the Confederates retired the assaulting column advanced. They covered the whole front of the valley between the fort and the town of Ironton, and, lapping over the slopes of Pilot Knob, formed

A Solid Line, Crescent Shaped,

the right half extending almost north and south, and the left half east and west. As soon as this great column made its appearance each piece of artillery in the fort was made to speak, and the Confederates were, in consequence, compelled to form their assaulting lines under fire. In this emergency the order to charge upon the fort was given without delay. While the column advanced all guns in the fort were brought to bear, and as the attacking party neared the fort the infantry and cavalry, that had retired from their positions early in the day, opened fire. The scene was of an interesting character. The little fort seemed to be belching forth sheets of flame. The artillery men stood to their guns and fought like demons. Now and then a gunner flinched, but officers stood by and rallied the men. Occasionally an artillery-man would express a desire to "get ammunition," but was dissuaded by the officer saying, "Stay up there; we'll keep you supplied." Every man able to fight was compelled to stand up and face the enemy. The assaulting column, after a brief fight, saw there was little chance of getting into the fort, as the ditch in front of it was so wide and deep as to form an impassable barrier, in view of the furious and unceasing fire. The first assault ended in the attacking party retiring a short distance, where they rallied and aided by fresh troops advanced again. The second attempt proved no more successful than the first, and the Confederates then drew off in the direction of the town of Pilot Knob, with the object of finding some weaker spot. This gave the infantry stationed in the ditch north of the fort a chance to get in some good work, which they improved, and the second assault, like the first, was a complete failure, the Confederates being repulsed. They effected but one lodgment, and that after retreating two miles to a point on the other side of Arcadia.

The Confederates left more than

Fifteen Hundred Dead and Wounded

on the battle-field. The Federal loss amounted to but ninety killed and wounded. The battle ended at 4 P.M., September 27, and less than an hour later the Federals began the work of removing their wounded to the town of Pilot Knob, although that place had been in the possession of the Confederates all day. The dead were buried in the fort, and preparations were made at once to abandon it, as by that time, Gen. Ewing had become convinced that its position was untenable. At midnight all the forces were withdrawn. Only the heavy guns and caissons were left behind, and this because there were no horses to draw them. Ewing's troops marched out of the fort, and as they passed between Shepherd and Rock Mountain they observed rebel camp fires and the sentries of a brigade that had taken up their position during the night. It was intended by Price that the intervening space between the camp fires and Rock Mountain should be filled by Shelby's division and orders had been sent to him to that effect. As Shelby moved down to comply with the orders his advance and Ewing's collided.

Postcard by Perkins Studio of the fort with survivors and the Ironton band wagon. *Missouri Department of Natural Resources Fort Davidson Collection, #65-2003-020-0001.*

Ewing, of course, was on the look-out, but Shelby was surprised, and as Ewing's forces advanced the enemy retreated. This was at a fork in the road, near the town of Caledonia. Ewing, seeing that he could not reach the Iron Mountain track, under the circumstances, took the road heading west, in the direction of the town of Webster, intending, if Price continued his march to St. Louis, in accordance with his previous announcement, to be in position to make a demonstration on Price's flank when opportunity offered. He soon discovered, however, that such a move would not be permitted, and that Price had ordered Gen. Clarke, commanding the Confederate cavalry, to pursue and bring him to battle. Ewing declined to give battle, however, and marched on to Leesburg, on the St. Louis and San Francisco railroad, erected breastworks there and prepared to give Price battle again. This for some reason Price declined, but instead, marched on towards Jefferson City, with the Federal force from St. Louis in pursuit.

Ewing Remained at Leesburg

three days, and then, under the escort of the 17th Illinois Cavalry, Col. Beveridge commanding, that had been sent from Rolla to his relief, he marched to the latter city and put his troops in garrison there under command of Col. Fletcher. He then returned to St. Louis with his staff by riding across country and taking the train from DeSoto to this point. Soon after Ewing's arrival here the order of Gen. Rosecrans above noted was issued.—*St. Louis Globe Democrat.*

Chapter 8
Pilot Knob Memorial Association Anniversary Booklets

The following pages are the three booklets that the Pilot Knob Memorial Association released between 1904 and 1906. Included are stories of the battle and information on particular survivors of the battle that has not been widely available to the public for more than one hundred years. Edited slightly for format but not for content. Any images used appear as they do in the original texts.

FROM THE MEETING OF THE PILOT KNOB MEMORIAL ASSOCIATION ON THE FORTIETH ANNIVERSARY OF THE BATTLE OF PILOT KNOB, SEPTEMBER 27, 1904. ORIGINALLY PRINTED BY PRESS A.R. FLEMING PRINTING COMPANY, ST. LOUIS, MISSOURI.

Brigadier General Thomas Ewing Jr., as he appeared forty years ago when commanding the one thousand hastily assembled Unionists who so gallantly and successfully defended Fort Davidson at the Battle of Pilot Knob, September 27, 1864.

INTRODUCTION AND HISTORICAL

The battle of Pilot Knob was fought on Sept. 27, 1865. The Union force consisted of a little more than 1000 men, commanded by Brig. Gen. Thos. Ewing Jr. The Confederate force was more than 20,000 men, commanded by Maj. Gen. Sterling Price.

Union loss, 15 killed, 11 mortally wounded, and 46 wounded who recovered.

Confederate loss, about 400 killed, 175 mortally wounded and more than 1000 wounded who recovered.

The casualty statistics show this to have been the most remarkable battle fought during the War of the Rebellion, when the great disparity in numbers engaged and losses incurred are compared.

After repulsing the repeated assaults of the Confederates, Gen. Ewing with his small force marched boldly through the enemy's lines and made a successful retreat to Leasburg, Mo., 61 miles away, in two days, checking the two cavalry divisions of the Confederates pursuing him with heavy loss, repeatedly as they attacked his rear in the last 20 miles of his retreat.

At Leasburg, Gen. Ewing was besieged for two days when a small body of troops came to his relief and the enemy dispersed or continued on the general raid across the state toward the Kansas line.

The small Union force hastily assembled at Pilot Knob under Gen. Ewing for the defense of that place consisted of detachments from seven regiments, 21 companies or parts of companies in all, with a few loyal citizens who took up arms and fought like veterans. These small organizations separated a few days after the battle not to meet again during the civil war, as they were returned to their several regimental organizations and served in different fields until the close of the strife. No *esprit du corps* had been established among these men before the battle and no time was given before their final separation for the waxing of a fraternal feeling commensurate with the hazards they had undergone together. After the war the survivors of the battle of Pilot Knob were still strangers to each other and being widely dispersed over the country when they returned to their homes a fraternal organization was not deemed possible and not attempted.

In the year 1882, on the 18th anniversary of the battle, such of the survivors as lived near the scene held a fraternal and memorial meeting in old Fort Davidson but no permanent organization was effected.

In the year 1900, a systematic course of looking up all survivors of the battle was begun by Dr. C.A. Peterson, of St. Louis, Mo.; with the view of collecting personal recollections and historic narratives from the participants and with the hope of bringing about a reunion of survivors on the 40th anniversary of the battle. As soon as this move was brought to the attention of Mr. Thomas Ewing, Jr., of Yonkers, New York, a son of Gen. Thomas Ewing, he heartily joined in the patriotic movement and contributed liberally of his time and means to raise the "great little battle" and its heoric [*sic*] survivors from unmerited obscurity and oblivion into the shining place they by right should occupy in history.

In 1903, after several hundred survivors of the battle had been definitely located, a meeting was held in St. Louis, Mo., on Oct. 6th, at the instance of Maj. H.B. Milks, of Leon, Kans., by the surviving participants of the battle and the Pilot Knob Memorial Association was duly organized and measures were at once begun to bring together on the 40th anniversary, Sept. 27th, 1904, every survivor of the battle, both Union and Confederate, who could possibly attend.

Fortieth Anniversary Reunion

At noontide on Monday, Sept. 26th, 1904, forty years after the opening of the battle to the exact hour, surviving participants from both armies, accompanied by hosts of their friends, began arriving in Arcadia Valley and assembling, as at a Mecca, in old Fort Davidson. The reunion continued until sundown Sept. 27th, which marked the closing hour of the battle just forty years before.

Old veterans who had taken a part in the terrific struggle for possession of this old earth-work forty years ago, were present from Texas, New Mexico, Oklahoma, Washington, Georgia, Kentucky, Arkansas, Illinois, Iowa, and Missouri, and interested visitors from every part of the Union. Among the latter perhaps the most interested and interesting were the sons and daughters of General Ewing, who at the time of the battle were small children or unborn babes. They had never before met the rugged men of the west whom their distinguished father had led forty years ago and it was a pathetic scene when they mingled with the mass of old soldiers, their children and grandchildren, forming brief, pleasant acquaintances amidst warm hand clasps and tears.

And among the old veterans the greetings and renewals of warm friendships severed forty years ago were not less affecting. Among these most warmly greeted by all of the old soldiers present were Col. David Murphy, who took such a gallant part in defending the fort and was aptly termed at the time "the Marshal Ney of Missouri" and Capt. William J. Campbell, the commander of the 14th Iowa Volunteers, who had stood like a granite wall with his handful of veteran infantry between the pursuing legions of Gen. Price and the small escaping command of Gen. Ewing on the long, arduous retreat to Leasburg on Sept. 28th and 29th, 1864, hurling back the Confederate cavalry divisions like chaff whenever they came in contact with his little band of invincibles. Grizzled old men flocked about Capt. Campbell, wrung his hand and wept, while they recalled the ordeal of forty years ago and recounted how he had made it possible that they should live and stand before him to-day.

Old Fort Davidson was a grim, barren, uninviting earth-work at the time of the battle; a stern instrument of war. To-day its outlines are mellowed by forty years of rain and sunshine. Its slopes and floor are covered with emerald sod and stately trees cast a gentle shade over the peaceful scene. In this inviting environment the men of blood and iron, of forty years ago, met each other, with their families and hosts of friends, to celebrate the blessings of peace and to commemorate the names of their noble comrades who laid down their lives, a willing sacrifice, on the altar of their country that freedom and liberty might not perish from the land.

More than one hundred survivors of the battle were present, with an equal number of old comrades in arms, and more than 1500 visiting friends, when at 2 p.m. Sept. 27th, as the clock marked the exact hour of the beginning of the grand assault on the fort forty years ago, the assemblage was called to order by Col. David Murphy, president of the Association, while the national emblem was hoisted to the inspiring air of "The Star Spangled Banner."

Rev. Wm. A. Meloan was introduced and offered the following invocation:

Our Father Who art in heaven, we come this blessed day, sacred in the memory of so many survivors of our battle, and we lift up our hearts in grateful thankfulness unto Thee for Thy tender mercies that have been offered us these forty years since we gathered together in this place on the day of battle and strife. We thank Thee, heavenly father, for the preservation of our lives, for the sweet comforts of home. We thank Thee for the life and development of a great Nation, which was baptized in the blood of our comrades. We praise Thee for every good thing in the world, because we know that Thou are the Giver of every good and perfect gift, and we know with Thee there is no variableness, neither shadow of turning. We thank Thee, O God, that thou art the same yesterday, to-day and forever: and that when Thou didst smile down upon the armies of that battle and bless them with victory Thou didst knit together their lives from the war, never to be separated, and that Thou art still with us lifting us to higher and, we trust, holier things.

We thank Thee, therefore, not only for the preservation of our lives, but we thank Thee for this sweet reunion. (Amen.) There comes to us this very moment memories that no heart nor tongue can tell: and O Lord, Thou art the Giver of these things and dost hold us in the hollow of Thy hand and abideth with us as a people, and hast preserved our lives all these years. A good many of us have come here our heads whitened with the winters of 40 years. And now, our Father, we pray Thy blessing upon this gathering. We pray Thy blessing upon this people, upon the Pilot Knob Memorial

Association, upon the old soldiers gathered here to-day to give glory, manhood and honor to this occasion. We ask Thee now, Heavenly Father, to bless this Association in the future, and God grant to keep us as long as there is use for us in the world. (Amen.)

Now, Father, we ask Thee when we go home with these comrades gathered here from all parts of this great country that they be in their homes an ever present blessing and may their children grow up around them and their grand-children to reverence them, in thankfulness for having overcome the hardships of our former days, and that they bear responsibilities of our great principles. We pray also that our last days may be our best days. (Amen.) And not only that we may be true soldiers of that great army who took part in that mighty struggle, but that we may be soldiers in the army of the Lord. (Amen.) And when that grand review shall come we pray that we may pass in robes of white before the great white throne of God, and receive from our Father in Heaven that welcome plaudit: "Well done thou good and faithful servant; thou hast been faithful over a few things, I will make thee ruler over many."

We now leave our loved ones, our comrades, our friends and our neighbors with Him, and pray that He will keep them in life, through Christ we ask it Amen.

Rev. Meloan introduced Col. David Murphy, in the following words:

Now comrades; we are going to have the honor of listening to an address from one who had as much to do possibly with the success that came to our arms here 40 years ago—because I call it a victory—as any man. I have the honor to introduce to you (although he needs no introduction, I should say, to the members of this Association) Col. David Murphy, the chief of artillery during the battle of Pilot Knob; and I seem to think I can hear those guns of his barking as he stands here today in our presence, and the shells whistling in the camp there, an instruction to our enemies, but not enemies today but friends and comrades who are with us here in this association. (Amen.)

Address of Col. David Murphy

Comrades, Ladies and Gentlemen: We had expected to have delivered on this occasion an address of welcome from one of the representative citizens of Pilot Knob or Ironton. But whether from modesty, or an innate desire on the part of those good people to avoid taking a conspicuous part in the ceremonies of the day, they have withheld their presence, cannot now be determined.

If we are spared, however, to take part in a future celebration of this day, we will see to it that these usual forms of courtesy shall be observed in a becoming manner.

But we do not need to have anybody say a good word for us: We are able to speak for ourselves as we did forty years ago, (Applause) without any help (Renewed applause). And now I want to say to you this: We have come all this way to meet with you and your families, and we have been permitted to listen to the eloquent comrade who has addressed the Throne of Grace asking God Almighty to look down upon us, and to bless us on this occasion, and the few remaining days that we have to live. After hearing that grand invocation, I feel like going home a better man than when I came here. (Amen.) And I hope that all the comrades who are here will say, whether they have been good or bad, "I will try from this day forward to be a better man." (Amen.)

Quite a number of those present know practically but little of the Battle of Pilot Knob. A large number have been born since the battle was fought.

True, it can be seen at a glance that one mountain of iron known as Pilot Knob stands on one side, and that another mountain of iron known as Shepherd Mountain stands on the other side, and other mountains on the remaining sides, and that there is now gathered together in our presence within the walls of Fort Davidson a large number of survivors of the battle with their families for the purpose of commemorating an event which occurred just forty years ago today. But the history of the battle has never been written; the young people growing up in southeast Missouri know but little of the stirring and portentious [sic] actions of that day. And yet, no history of the Civil War or of the struggle for the maintenance of the Union and the defeat of secession can be considered as complete without a full narrative of the important part played and the far-reaching results attained by those who took part in the defense of Pilot Knob.

I will not attempt in the short time allowed me at this time to narrate all the events of that day, or make any effort at details, but will cursorily refer to the salient points descriptive of the battle and the events which preceded and followed the same.

It was the latter part of September, 1864. Sherman was at Atlanta, Georgia, which place he had entered September 2nd. He was making preparations to leave that city behind him in his march to the sea. Thomas was at Nashville, awaiting an attack from the Confederate General Hood, who had relieved General Joe Johnston on the 17th of the month and was then in the northern part of Alabama, searching for a weak point in the Union lines to attack. The Confederate General Kirby Smith, then commanding the Trans-

Mississippi department, with headquarters at Shreveport, conferred with General Sterling Price of Missouri as to the feasibility of making an invasion of Missouri, then almost depleted of regular volunteer troops, marching upon St. Louis, capturing that important and wealthy city, securing the vast arsenal of ordnance stores, quartermaster and commissary supplies, together with such gold, silver and U.S. currency as could be captured by a rapid movement upon the city. After that, there was the large extent of country lying just east of St. Louis, Southern Illinois and Indiana, both of which were overrun with secret societies inimical to the U.S. Government. The Knights of the Golden Circle and other secret oath-bound organizations existed in the southern portion of those states and with a strong force of their friends, the Confederate Army, it was believed that they could create such a scare at Washington as to force a hasty withdrawal of Sherman from Atlanta and Thomas from Nashville to save the invaded states north of the Ohio river from becoming the new theatre of war.

General Price left Camden, Ark., on the 28th of August with the divisions of Generals Fagan and Marmaduke, consisting of fourteen thousand veteran cavalry and ten pieces of artillery. He crossed the Arkansas river on September 6th at Dardanelle and marched to Pocahontas, where he was joined by another division of ten thousand men and four pieces of artillery under General Joe Shelby. The three divisions invaded Missouri, marching by parallel roads with orders to form a junction at Fredericktown, 22 miles east of Pilot Knob, by the 24th of September. The junction was made as ordered and immediately General Shelby was ordered to move northwardly via Farmington to Mineral Point and then destroy the bridges on the Iron Mountain Railroad and cut off the retreat of the little garrison at Pilot Knob and prevent them from reaching St. Louis, thus, as General Price supposed, insuring the capture of Ft. Davidson with its armament and stores.

General W.S. Rosecrans, commanding the Union forces in Missouri, had been advised of the contemplated movements of the invading army, and made his dispositions so as to protect every strategic point in his department. Jefferson City, Rolla, St. Louis and other garrisons were reinforced by the calling in of the scattered troops and forces under his command, and the question in the mind of the department commander was, whether to call in the garrison at Pilot Knob, or let it remain and "hold the fort." General Thomas Ewing, commander of the St. Louis District, was ordered to Pilot Knob with instructions to hold the place against any detached force, but his further orders were, that if he was satisfied that Price was in his front with his entire force, he (Ewing) should blow up the magazine of the fort and retire on St. Louis.

Upon the arrival of General Ewing at this place he at once ordered all the stores of the quartermaster and commissary department to be moved to St. Louis. This was done on the 26th. On the same day some of the wagon guards returned and reported to General Ewing the loss of teams and stores by a large force operating between Pilot Knob and St. Louis. On the same day his pickets in the Arcadia Valley, to the south, were driven in and the reinforcements sent to their aid were also driven back upon the slope of Pilot Knob and Shepherd Mountain. Then it was that General Ewing determined to prepare for the worst. It was not known how strong a force had driven in his reinforced pickets, and the question for him to decide was: Is General Price with his entire force in my front? There was a hasty consultation with the leading officers, not a council of war, but separate interviews with the different commanders; and it was finally decided that the fort should be held on the morrow until night, if possible; and if it was developed in the battle that the entire Confederate force was present, a retreat would be ordered and that the best policy was to make a stiff fight preliminary to an attempt at a retreat.

On the morning of the 27th of September the fighting was renewed, at this time on the slopes of Shepherd Mountain and Pilot Knob. Later in the morning our troops were driven into the fort and Marmaduke's artillery planted on the eastern face of Shepherd Mountain commanding the fort. (A call was here made for three cheers for General Ewing, which were given).

Well, as I said, they got four pieces of artillery right up here on the mountain top, as much as to say: "We've got you now!" and General Ewing himself felt that we were in a very precarious position, and he said to me: "Why don't you open fire, don't you see them planting their battery up there?" I was in charge of the artillery in the fort, and I answered: "Yes, I see them planting their artillery there, but," I said, "you know that we have decided to hold this fort until night, and if they want to keep off their fire until night, let them do so; I am not going to precipitate this battle." I had in mind the incident of the French guards at Fontenoy under Louis XIV. When they came in position before the English force, the French commander stepped out of the ranks, took off his hat and said: "Gentlemen of the English guards, fire!" And the commander of the English guards said: "No! the English guards always receive the first fire." I told him then: "We will let them fire the first gun, and they can't say they are not ready; they can't say we have taken advantage of them. But as soon as they open on us with their gun fire, then these guns from the western side of the fort shall reply." From Marmaduke's guns came the first fire and in less than 20 minutes that battery was driven from its chosen position and dragged down to the shoulder of the mountain beyond there out of the way. That was the first taste of victory, because we had disposed of the most seriously threatening feature of the attack, the artillery fire from Shepherd Mountain.

Then came the rebel assaulting column from the direction of Ironton pouring up from over Pilot Knob and Shepherd Mountain 12,000 armed men, coming in one grand body. They seemed to be drunk with the prospect of victory, as if to say: "We will walk right over them and sweep them out of the way." Oh, but they didn't walk over us; they didn't sweep us out of their way. We swept them back, and they never stopped until they were two miles away. All their chance of victory was gone. Their loss in the battle was a little less than 1500 men killed and wounded. After the battle was over, and after our men had cheered themselves hoarse and were resting after their arduous work, a little incident occurred right over there where that tent stands: There was a colored man lying on his back. I knew him very well; we had treated him as the captain of the colored contingent that had helped to put this fort in a condition for the defense. He lay there and says I: "Captain Jim, you must get up; this is no time to be lying down; get up, because we are getting ready to go out." He says: "I can't get up, I am mortally wounded." I asked him where, and he said he was shot through the hips. Says I: "I will see that you are taken care of." Says he: "Never mind me, Major; when I look up and see the old flag floating, and victory perching over our little band, I die content." (Applause).

That was the same sentiment, and that was the same spirit that actuated the white defenders of Pilot Knob. I took him over to the hospital, helped to carry him myself, and placed him under the charge of Dr. Carpenter, who had very hard work to keep his color from being discovered and his body taken out and mutilated by the infuriated rebels when they entered the town; but he was not discovered, and he was buried as a faithful, loyal citizen should be buried; he was given the burial of a good union soldier.

Then, as we marched out, we went up through this gorge and on to Caledonia. There we met the terrible Shelby coming down, all his men swearing and gritting their teeth, and imagining to themselves the number of men they were going to kill when they got down here. Well, our little advance dashed into their advance and we captured three or four of them and drove the others back, and they fell back to Shelby and said: "A.J. Smith! Where did he come from?" "Don't know." "Form line of battle," he says, "A.J. Smith is here." And whilst he was forming his line of battle, General Ewing, like a good, sensible general, turned to the left and marched his command of 600 men, all that was left of his little command, on toward Webster. While the terrible Shelby had formed his men in line of battle waiting to be attacked by A.J. Smith, and never knew the difference until General Price marched up from Pilot Knob and asked him what he was doing. Says he: "I am waiting for Smith." "Smith, you fool, is not here. Where is Ewing?" "I don't know; he must have gone to the west." "Well, get after him, get after him." (Laughter).

But Shelby was not very anxious to overtake the little command; he didn't want to meet the men that had fought at Pilot Knob. If he could have gotten some poor lone merchant to come out of his store, without a gun in his hand, or perhaps a farmer militiaman with a Federal uniform on, he would have killed him in his tracks without giving him time to pray. That is the kind of enemy that Shelby liked to meet, but not men like those that fought at Pilot Knob. And they followed us for many miles; they had two mounted divisions, 7,000 strong, and seven pieces of artillery, and when Ewing would halt and prepare for battle, the pursuing force would halt, and so it was for 60 miles that they followed us to Leasburg. There we threw up some slight works. Some accounts of the campaign declare that the enrolled militia had constructed these works, but you all know that we built them ourselves, using railroad ties as the foundation, covering them with earth, and we stood again, just as we stood at Pilot Knob, and said: "Come on." Did they come on? No, they stood there and parleyed and counted the cost: "How many men will it cost to take that little band of 600? We have only got 7,000; how many of our men will have to bite the dust if we take those terrible little fighters from Pilot Knob?" Well, they said the fortifications were too formidable; they were afraid of those fortifications; it wasn't the men, you know. Well, as a matter of fact, you could have kicked those fortifications down with your foot. It was the boldest bluff ever perpetrated upon a demoralized and defeated foe, but it was sufficient; the bluff worked; the fortifications were too formidable, and the great Marmaduke, and the terrible Shelby, the Napoleon of the South, marched off and left us there alone at Leasburg, with the loss of only a few men. Why? Why, it was because the soldiers of Pilot Knob had taught these men that if they made an attack upon them they would give them the worst of it.

Do you remember during that time of the war, that the army of the South was induced to invade Pennsylvania? The men were assured that they would have to fight only the Pennsylvania militia. "If we go up there, we will whip them. Yes, we can whip the Pennsylvania militia, and let us do it." This was at Gettysburg; and after fighting a three days battle on the heights of Gettysburg, the men of the South exclaimed: "Why this is the army of the Potomac." They were victims of misplaced confidence. And they wanted to fight no more; it was too much for them.

That is the way it was with our little band at Leasburg; we were too much for the 7,000 men under Generals Price, Marmaduke, Cabell and Shelby.

That is the way the battle of Pilot Knob was fought, and the successful retreat to Leasburg. That is the way the glorious record was made. And now, for the resulting consequence of the determined stand made by General Ewing and his command at Pilot Knob:

From Leasburg, on the "Frisco" road, Price's army marched unopposed to Jefferson City, the capital of the state, which was fortified and well garrisoned with seasoned troops under Generals Fisk and Brown.

Upon reaching that place General Price viewed the fortification and shook his head, evidently remembering Pilot Knob, and passed on, leaving it unattacked. He marched on to Boonville, which was defended by some citizen militia, who, when summoned, surrendered, and there General Price won his first GLORIOUS victory in Missouri. From there he marched through the secession counties of Saline, Lafayette and Jackson to the vicinity of Westport, where the Kansas citizen militia were strung out in an extended line to protect their state from invasion, and to prevent the repetition of such scenes as were enacted at Lawrence, Kansas, in 1863.

There, Price was engaged for several days making but little headway until the cavalry forces under Generals Pleasanton, Brown, McNeil and Colonel Benteen overtook him, and then began the wild retreat from Missouri to Arkansas, leaving behind him in his train, his artillery, many of his men prisoners, defeated in every aim and purpose which he had hoped for on entering the state. By the action of General Ewing in making the stand at Pilot Knob and his movement westwardly, he drew General Price after him in pursuit and thus the city of St. Louis was saved from assault, and possibly destruction, and Jefferson City was untouched. The states of Illinois and Indiana were left undisturbed, and Generals Sherman and Thomas were allowed to carry out their part in the closing period of the war which resulted in the defeat of Generals Hood and Joe Johnston and the fall of Richmond. And all of these grand results may reasonably be ascribed to the gallant defense of Pilot Knob on the 27th day of September, 1864.

And now, my friends, in conclusion, let me ask you to think of these events as illustrative of the battle of life: We may meet difficulties and troubles which we may deem too serious to overcome; our enemies may appear to be too numerous, too well organized to resist; we may ask ourselves "Whether it is nobler in the mind to suffer the slings and arrows of outrageous fortune, or to take arms against a sea of troubles and by opposing them, end them." And then, by bravery, faithfulness, vigilance and patriotism overcome the obstacles, and overcome the embarrassments. Let every man, young man, every woman and child, boy and girl here, as they pass through life, say: "I was at Pilot Knob and I heard the speaker tell about the battle, and I heard him speak of the bravery of the thousand men within those grounds, who stood and dared the assault of 20,000 men under General Price; and I heard him tell how the enemy advanced in glorious array, and how the little band of 1,000 swept them back like a besom of destruction, and they went back crushed, defeated and disheartened."

"So, I," speaking for these young men, "will take this as a lesson; I will honor these brave men, and when trouble comes up before me, I will stand fast, and when I am overtaken by a sea of troubles, and when everything seems impossible to bear, I will sweep everything back and come out gloriously victorious as did the brave defenders of Pilot Knob." (Applause).

(A call for three cheers for Colonel Murphy was made and given).

Colonel Murphy then introduced Mr. Thomas Ewing, Jr., as follows:

Now, my friends and comrades, I have another pleasant duty to perform. General Ewing has left a family who revere his memory. The entire family have come all the way from New York to see the men who stood by their father when he fought at Pilot Knob. I will now introduce to you Thomas Ewing, Jr., the son of our gallant general, who led us in that great battle.

(Three cheers were asked for General Ewing and given).

ADDRESS OF THOMAS EWING, JR.

I thank you, Colonel Murphy, and ladies and gentlemen and particularly the survivors of this battle, for your warm reception given to me as the representative of my father. I have been selected from among his five children, who are all out here today, to say a few words, mainly to tell you that we are glad to be here. It would not be fitting for me to make an address. I knew nothing of the battle except from my father's lips, and there are more than 100 men here who took part. They are the ones who should be heard from; they are the ones to lend interest by telling what they saw on that notable occasion.

There is one little incident, however, which I would like to relate as a companion piece to the touching story told by Colonel Murphy, of Captain Jim. During the fight, at a time when there was a lull in the attack on the fort, my father was moving around noting the conditions at different points. In the ditch he found a boy of 16 or 17 years of age; his eyes were shut, his face pale, and he was evidently very near his end. My father reached down and tried to lift him out of the ditch. The boy opened his eyes and said:

"Oh, General, never mind me, never mind me." My father, in telling the story, used to say that he could still see the look of pride which lighted up the boy's face when he saw who it was trying to help him.

(Three cheers were again asked for General Ewing and given).

It was characteristic, I think, of our armies that there was much initiative on the part of the individual member; and this was true of the little band gathered here during the terrible days, forty years ago. They were not commanded by a West Pointer; they were commanded by one who had seen comparatively little service; some of them were men of far more active service in warfare than he. All did their part, and it was the fight of all. But I am reminded that after Marathon, the reward granted to Miltiades was that on the picture representing the battle his image was placed first among the Athenians. That is all I ask as a recognition of my father's service here. It was a grand little army, and you made a grand fight; but you were led by a grand commander.

(Three cheers were again asked for General Ewing, and were given).

Colonel Murphy introduced Mr. William C. Ewing:

"Now, comrades and friends, I am going to introduce to you another son of General Ewing, who looks more like him than the one who has spoken here. This is William Ewing, another son of General Ewing:

Address of William C. Ewing

I am glad to see you here, ladies and gentlemen, and I am glad to come back again and meet some of those who were at this fort forty years ago when it was complete and the magazine was in place before Price came up and spoiled it. I saw the fort in the summer of 1864 with its embankment and drawbridge and the log magazine covered with a mound of earth, at a time when there was little anticipation that an action would be fought here that should make it famous. I am glad to come back and say a word to you. As my brother has said more fully, the family of General Ewing are grateful for the reception we have met, and we appreciate the recollection that the people of this neighborhood have of the little fight that was fought here and the estimation in which it is held by the State of Missouri and by the people of the neighboring states. It was a little fight, but in its spirit and in its force, and in the magnitude of its results it was one of the great minor fights of the war, and we are all proud of our inheritance in it, as all those must be who had a part in it themselves or in the persons of their friends or relatives. I thank you for your attention.

Address of Rev. Wm. A. Meloan

I do not need to say that I feel perfectly happy in being in this presence today. I feel that God has been good to me, that after forty years I have been permitted once more to look into the faces of at least the remnant of those brave men who stood here and did their duty to God and to their country. I stand before you as the representative of the units of this battle; I was not one of the representative leaders; I was not in the council of war; I was not permitted to enter into the knowledge of the details of this battle that resulted in so much good to our side and to our nation; but I was here as a simple sergeant in Company A of the Third Cavalry, which was never known to fail in the presence of the enemy or quail before the hail of musketry. And I stand here, therefore, as the representative of the private soldier, that part of the machine that carries out the work of the brain and without which the brain would work in vain. And I want, therefore, for you to recognize the fact that you have had just as much part in this battle and in the victory that came to us upon that day as the chiefest men that stood here and led you to victory and glory. (Amen). Only because the private was behind the gun, and because the private aimed the shot that carried destruction up yonder, all that patriotism would have been in vain. I believe in giving honor to whom honor is due. I believe in profound reverence for the leaders that God gave us in the great conflict, who knew how to so direct our stroke that we might accomplish great things for our nation. I wish I was an artist; I would paint a picture of this beautiful valley forty years ago; I would try to impress upon the minds, when I met some of the forces scattered here and there, as I saw them simply as one down in the ranks trying to work out my part of the work given me to do; and I would make that picture after the battle was on; I would take a point over here on this spur on Shepherd Mountain, and over there, you would see on the spur of Shepherd Mountain the 14th Iowa Infantry—grand men as ever walked beneath the starry flag—led by their invincible commander who had been in many battles, true veterans and tried, and they stood over there before the mighty forces that came sweeping up the valley and holding them there tenaciously. Over yonder on the side of Pilot Knob was that man whom I venerate more than any man that stood connected with this battle; I mean the brave, patriotic, unfailing Wilson. (Cheers). Leading his men behind him, standing like a stone wall, hurling back the forces that were bearing against him, until decimated, felled and scattered, he was captured by the enemy. And never did an enemy shoot a braver man than when they shot Major Wilson. It was the fortunes of war. That was the condition over there; and by and by, it seemed out of flame and smoke up yonder on the side of Shepherd Mountain, a shell came, or something came, shrieking down here into this fort. I said to myself, with blanched face, it may be the end has come to us now. And then I saw hurried work over there; our chief of artillery, whom God has spared to be with us today, trained his gun upon that battery and in twenty minutes it was gone from its place in the angry flame as the battle ceased.

You all know then that a great array came starting up; that great array of men about which he talked, with banners flying, with all their forces of might and power, to sweep out of the way this little band of heroic men that had dared to place themselves in the way of the mighty advancing army.

Then I saw another sight that thrills my blood as I tell it now: I saw this man we call Colonel Murphy today, standing right there simply with his hat in his hand, and he trained those guns, and I thought: What a man is that! We called him "Old Murphy" then; they call him that yet. (Laughter). He was about 28 years old. And Murphy's guns began again, and the next time I got a good sight of the thing that whole plain was swept away; and, with the exception of one thing, I am sad to day, the dead and the dying, the shrieks of the dying, the plain was littered with the remnant of those left behind when that mighty array of strength swept back beyond Ironton two miles from us, and victory perched upon our banners once more.

My beloved, we can realize it: I have told some of these people since I have been in your midst that I have tried to study the inscrutable ways of Divine Providence, and I have never yet been able to understand it. I told that to a confederate soldier; I reckon he will forgive me if I tell a joke he got off. I believe he says it is all right. Last night I said: "I don't see how you people ever managed on earth to let us slip through your fingers." "Why," he says, "you don't understand, we were perfectly willing for you to leave as you were to go." (Laughter). Perfectly willing! Well, I will tell you, my brethren, I am going to compromise; I am going to say that for the good of our country and in order, too, that brave men might not have died, we were perfectly willing to stop just then. And, I am going a little further: We didn't stop until we got ready to stop and were willing to stop.

Now, my friends, Mr. William Ewing said that he looked upon this fort before it was dismantled by General Price. I want to tell all the people here that General Price did not dismantle this fort; we dismantled it ourselves before we left. Now, Brother Ewing, you will please remember that; we blew that fort up and we left nothing here but our dead, precious dead, and our wounded. Now, at the edge of the fort we laid the dead. I don't know whether true or not, but I have since heard when it was blown up the earth was blown over them, and that is their grave today. I don't know but what that is the most precious place in which they could have been buried. (Amen). It is here that they died; it is here that their spirit took its flight to that beautiful land that lies across the dark river of death. It was here that they had worked out the great work of their life; it was here that they answered the call of duty; it was here that they obeyed officers that a nation had placed over them; it was here that they as simple units—I want you to remember that, after the great multitude that went to form the Grand Army of this nation—they dared to do and did do even to death; and if they sleep here in this site it is a blessed sleep, a sleep to be awakened from clothed in the brightness of that resurrection morn when God will clothe them in beautiful white and reunite them over at the gate, because I am one of those preachers who believes that every man who was brave enough to die for his country is good enough to go to heaven. (Amen, and applause).

And I told a lot of those boys of the Illinois and Iowa; I talked to 5,000 of them at one time in McDonough County and preached to them of Christian manhood, and said to them that I was prepared to shrive their souls right then and they could tell any kind of war stories they pleased and they would all be forgiven and they could go home without sin.

Now, comrades, of course I had no part in this battle any more than that of any other comrade; I was the least governed man of any of them in that war. I said they were going to end the balance of the fight, but it was not to be so. In the wee small hours of the night the council of brain was going on, and they had finally decided, Colonel Murphy, they would obey orders. That is the first time I ever heard anybody putting off obeying orders two days; if we did not we would enter the guard house.

I revere the memory of General Ewing today for that more than anything else that he did, and I want to tell his children that I thank God that he did disobey orders that time and that he did not vacate this fort and leave us to be massacred by the enemy. (A call for three cheers for General Ewing was made and given).

I tell you, my men, I know something about it: I belonged to Company A of the Third M.S.M. Cavalry under Major James Wilson. There was as good a man as the Third had, and they hadn't anything but good men. And we had made up our minds that we would never surrender, because we knew the result. I told him when I found out that [the] leaders were going to surrender: We will go to the woods; and we knew every by-path in this country; we knew every hog track in this country; we knew every gatepost and fence in this country; and we could have gone out in the foothills and the mountains and stayed there for weeks in spite of all the army that Price or any other general could have brought into this country. I tell you, the old Third was prepared on that occasion to take care of herself. Brethren, you will forgive me for saying something about my nation. I wouldn't give a cent for a man that didn't love his country; I wouldn't give anything for a man that didn't love his home; I wouldn't give anything for a man that didn't love the army in which he made a part; I wouldn't give anything for a man that didn't love his regiment, and I wouldn't give the slip of my finger for a man who didn't think his company and his officers were the best ones in the whole regiment. That is the way I feel about it, my comrades.

Now then, I want to say as to one of the changes that has taken place these blessed years. It has been forty years since I stood in this fort, a mere beardless youth, and don't forget that, you old men. I didn't do very much, I know; but I will tell you what I did. I did like the story of the woman in the scripture; she did what she could. (Amen). That is all anybody can do. I did my part, and that is something; whatever the consequences was and the benefits from the battle, our names will be enrolled and our memories will be enshrined in faithful bosoms, and embalmed in loving hearts, and we will be remembered and not forgotten by a grateful nation.

Now, my beloved, we are here again once more after forty years. I have been battling—I must preach a little—in another army. Thirty years ago I enlisted in the army of the Lord. Thirty-two years ago I was ordained as a minister of the Gospel, and from that time to this I have had two flags that I love better than anything else: I love the starry flag, our nation's emblem, the most beautiful flag that ever kissed the breezes of Heaven, and the one that represents the grandest principles and the holiest truth, and that is life, liberty and the pursuit of happiness to all men: I love it. And, by the side of and above it, I have gotten another flag. It is upon a snow-white cloth with a blood-red cross, and in that blood-red cross of Christ I have been trying to win my comrades and my neighbors and the people to march under those two flags until God shall call them from labor to rest. (Amen). And, my comrades, when I leave you I am going back to that same work again, and if God permit me to be with you any more I will come back here and speak again about the glorious things which have been spoken of to you, and how you have been remembered by the people. And I want to say just one other word. This battle has never been appreciated by the people of the country; this battle has never been appreciated by the representative men of the nation; and I am going to add something to that, if you will permit me. I was a Southern-born man; I was born under slavery, if you want me to put it that way. I was taught that it was by divine right, and all that sort of thing, and a great many other fictions that have faded out of my brain. That was the condition, and I will tell you something else now to keep part with what Colonel Murphy has stated to you; that from the South was the test of flesh and blood and the inheritance of years and associations of life, but we stood by the flag of our country. (Amen, and applause). This nation has never yet honored the Southern Union soldier as he has a right to be honored. (That is right). He is here today to say just a word or two in his defense. If I am right in my statistics, there were nearly 500,000 men that enlisted in the Union army from the South. Now, then, there were 2,200,000 in the Federal army from beginning to end, and there were 875,000 in the Southern army; and I have often tried to figure out, and as one of my old friends tried to figure out, what would have been the result if these 500,000 men had been led by its flesh and blood and the associations and by inheritance and all that, and had gone with the South, then it would have been 1,370,000 pitted against 1,700,000, and I don't know what would have happened, but I know that Old Glory would never have been trailed in the dust. Still it would have made difficulties. My friends, let us ever thank the living and the dead. (Amen).

Now, I tell you, our comrades and friends, we had brothers on the one side, brothers on the other, and we had neighbors on one side and neighbors on the other; we had a glorious time in going home; we sneaked in at the back door, and when the night time came we went out in the fields and slept with our revolvers at our side to protect ourselves, and when morning came and the streets had taken on some of the beautiful yellow, we stepped out the front door. That was the situation you can understand. And I stand here the representative of the Southern young man who had as bloody a story in the records of the State of Missouri as any other man in this goodly land of ours.

Now, just one word and I am done. How shall we keep good the memory of these men? I will tell you how we can keep their memories; we can keep their memories by perpetuating the principles upon which this country was founded. Our fathers said that all men are right free and equal and they have certain inalienable rights that cannot be taken from them, such as life, liberty and the pursuit of happiness. I am going to say to you, comrades, and to your children, that this country guarantees to every man living, freedom before the law, and that it guarantees to every man security of life and of property and the pursuit of happiness, and that he may pursue it so he does not destroy the happiness of his fellow man. And when we are true to these principles we will be true to our old flag, and when we are true to that we will be true to God.

And now I will make an invocation for you: I pray God to take care of you, to watch your steps as you go home, and to keep you from the path of evil and direct you.

And now, believe me, comrades, if you will be true to yourselves, God will be true to you; and after life's labor is ended and you have fought your last battle and you breathe out your spirit and it goes up to God who gives it, that you will have the grandest triumph and the grandest victory that ever came to man. You will be seated upon the right hand of the Majesty on high and you will reign there in fadeless grandeur and rejoice in deathless love.

(Three cheers were given for Comrade Meloan).

ADDITIONAL REMARKS BY COL. DAVID MURPHY

Comrades and Friends: I want to say a word or two to you about this organization of the Pilot Knob Memorial Association. As its name would indicate, we have formed this association for the purpose of commemorating the services of those who fought here, and commemorating the memory of those who died under the Stars and Stripes. You will notice that so far as we are concerned, you have not been called on to contribute one cent of expense of this meeting. You have been protected by the officers of this association in this place from any game of chance; none has been permitted or allowed inside of the grounds. Money has been offered us if we would only grant the privilege and we denied it. No, we will have no games of chance, no skin games here for our own beloved people. Now, we propose to go further, and we propose to continue this organization, if the people of southeast Missouri will help by raising money enough to buy this ground and dedicate it to the memory of those who fell in battle here. Now, that is a grand object and a grand purpose, and we hope if the friends who have been here today will continue to give us their assistance and their influence in the completion of it, we can consummate this great work.

EXECUTIVE MEETING

A business session of the Association was then held and the following officers were elected to serve one year, after which the meeting adjourned to September 27, 1905:

Officers of the Pilot Knob Memorial Association.
DAVID MURPHY, President, St. Louis, Mo.
H.C. WILKINSON, Secretary, Piedmont, Mo.
C.A. PETERSON, Corresponding Secretary, St. Louis, Mo.
HENRY S. CARROLL, Treasurer, St. Louis, Mo.

Vice-Presidents:
Wm. J. Campbell, Oakville, Iowa.
H.B. Milks, Leon, Kan.
Sam B. Rowe, Rolla, Mo.
T.M. Montgomery, Akard, Mo.
Wm. H. Smith, Park Place, Ore.
James W. Nations, Womack, Mo.
Eli D. Ake, Ironton, Mo.

Assistant Secretaries:
Hugo Hoffbauer, Buffalo, Iowa.
John a. Rice, Braswell, Mo.
John H. Delano, Murphysboro, Ill.
James C. Steakley, Patton, Mo.
Charles Biehle, St. Louis, Mo.
James M. Travis, Greenfield, Mo.
Thos. Ewing, Jr., 67 Wall St., New York, N.Y.

SURVIVORS PRESENT AT THE REUNION

Fourteenth Iowa Infantry

Capt. Wm. J. Campbell, Co. K Comdg. Regt.	Oakville, Ia.
Lieut. Hugo Hoffbauer, Co. A. Regtl. Adjt.	Buffalo, Ia.
Corpl. Edwin H. Tyler, Co. B Color Bearer	Nashua, Ia.
John Birk, Co. H	Anamosa, Ia.

Third M.S.M. Cavalry

Co. A, Sergt. Wm. A. Meloan	Elsberry, Mo.
" Henry H. Ashbaugh	Starkdale, Mo.
" Frederick W. Page	Elsberry, Mo.
" Wm. L.H. Silliman	Clarksville, Mo.
" John H. Wynn	Piedmont, Mo.
" Co. C, Capt. John W. Hendrick	BowlingGreen, Mo.
" Sergt. John L. Cole	Louisiana, Mo.
Co. D, Sergt. Wm. F. Pritchett	Vandalia, Mo.
" James H. Brown	Olney, Mo
" Aylette F. Butler	Marling, Mo.
" Frank Butler	New Hartford, Mo.
" Lorenzo D. Davis	Couch, Mo.
" Isaac H. Dillon	Marling, Mo.
" Abraham M. Lafferty	Middleton, Mo.
" Enoch M. Layerty	Garber, Okla. Ter.
" Ferdinand O. Tennison	Elvins, Mo.
" Wm. N. Vannoy	Vandalia, Mo.
Co. H, Capt. Henry B. Milks	Leon, Kans.
" Lieut. John P. Rogers	Montgomery, Mo.
" Sergt. Wm. Y.M. Wilkerson	Jonesboro, Ark.
" Corpl.Wm. H. Cameron	Warrenton, Mo.
" Henry Anderson	Hickman, Ky.
" Elijah Evans	Avon, Mo.
" Wm. Z. Evans	Avon, Mo.
" John Norman	Couch, Mo.
" John Tumilty	Bowling Green, Mo.
Co. I, Lieut. Warren C. Shattuck	Vandalia, Mo.
" John M. Grover	Hamberg, Ill.
" George W. Rhodes	Glen Allen, Mo.
" Artemus L. Shattuck	Vandalia, Mo.
" Charles K. Tinnin	Fredericktown, Mo.
" Wash. Underwood	Higdon, Mo.
Co. K, Ephrian Hasty	Arcadia, Mo.
" Joseph W. Myers	Husky, Mo.
" John W. Ragsdale	East St. Louis, Mo.
" Samuel Rhodes	Glen Allen, Mo.

" James G. Roe   Piedmont, Mo.
" Alfred Shell   Hahn, Mo.

Second M.S.M. Cavalry

Co. L, Lieut. John A. Rice   Alton, Mo.
" John Parkin   Belgrade, Mo.

First M.S.M. Infantry

Co. G, Adolph Dick   Clarksburg, Mo.
" George Suess   Miami Station, Mo.

Second Mo. Light Artillery

Battery H, Alfred J. Hazelton   McCloud, Okla. Ter.

Forty-seventh Mo. Infantry

Lieut. David Murphy, Regtl. Adjt.
Comdg. Art   St. Louis, Mo.
Sergt. Maj. John H. Delano   Murphysboro, Ill.
Qr. Mr. Sergt. Samuel B. Rowe   Rolla, Mo.

Co. A, Sergt. C.B.L. Rowland   Greenville, Mo.
" Sergt. Salathial A. Harris   Patterson, Mo.
" Sergt. E.B. Sawyer   Munger, Mo.
" Wm. H. Burmingham   Greenville, Mo.
" John Wesley Evans   Lodi, Mo.
Co. E, Lieut. John Schwab   Ironton, Mo.
" David Borders   Green River, Mo.
" William A. Fletcher   Arcadia, Mo.
" George Pinkley   Lutesville, Mo.
" Frederick Rodach   Middlebrook, Mo.
Co. F, Corpl. Thomas Lang   Farmington, Mo.
" John Copeland   Ellington, Mo.
" Francis M. Gaulding   Couch, Mo.
" E.K. Hopkins   Farmington, Mo.
" Wm. F. Miller   Farmington, Mo.

" Wm. M. Murphy	Tucumcari, New Mex.
Co. G, Lieut. James E. Davis	Fredericktown, Mo.
" Sergt. J.C. Paullus	Belleview, Mo.
" J.S. Bennett	Piedmont, Mo.
" Isaac I. Bounds	Greenville, Mo.
" Hardin Garner	St. Louis, Mo.
" Joel K.P. Wood	Irondale, Mo.
Co. H, Sergt. Henry C. Wilkinson	Piedmont, Mo.
" Henry E. Goad	Brunot, Mo.
" Azariah Martin	Ironton, Mo.
Co. I, Sergt. Jacob M. Rhodes	Fredericktown, Mo.
" Wm. Holly	Mine La Motte, Mo.
" Jesse F. Inman	Roselle, Mo.
" Thomas J. Rice	Des Loge, Mo.
" Peter Shrum	Sligo, Mo.
" Joseph Wood	Mine La Motte, Mo.

Fiftieth Mo. Infantry

Co. E., Thos. Fortune	Caledonia, Mo.
" James A. Rives	Piedmont, Mo.
Co. F. Joseph F. Lindsay	Piedmont, Mo.
" Wm. H. Musgrove	Marquand, Mo.
" James W. Nations	Womack, Mo.
" Benjamin Woodruff	Hendrickson, Mo.

Citizens' Defense Organization

Wm. T. Leeper	Leeper, Mo.
Dr. G.W. Farrar, Sr. Vol. Surgeon	Ironton, Mo.
Willis Cole	Ironton, Mo.
Thomas T. Dalton	Farmington, Mo.
Daniel B. Dyer	Augusta, Ga.
Herman Davis	Ironton, Mo.
James Ellis	Pilot Knob, Mo.
Peter Gerstenmeyer	Pilot Knob, Mo.
Frederick Kaths	Pilot Knob, Mo.
Crume K. Miller	Kirkwood, Mo.

John W. Perry	North Alton, Ill.
George Patterson	Patterson, Mo.
Henry Valle	Ironton, Mo.

Ex-Confederate Survivors Present

Josiah T. Blanton, Co. C 9th Mo. Inft. C.S.A.	Ironton, Mo.
Richard Collins, Co. F 1st Mo. Inft. C.S.A.	Fredericktown, Mo.
Peter Carnahan, Co. C 3rd Mo. Cav. C.S.A.	Arcadia, Mo.
D.L. Glaves, Bat. A 4th Mo. Lt. Art. C.S.A.	Fredericktown, Mo.
John H. Harper, Co. A 4th Mo. Cav. C.S.A.	Bloomfield, Mo.
Alexander Moore, Co. A 3rd Mo. Cav. C.S.A.	Farmington, Mo.
Joseph J. Moyer, Co. A 1st Mo. Cav. C.S.A.	Caledonia, Mo.
Wm. A. Moyer, Co. A 1st Mo. Cav. C.S.A.	Caledonia, Mo.
John F. Peak, Battery A 1st Ark. Art. C.S.A.	Graniteville, Mo.
Andrew J. Rayburn, Co. C 10th Mo. Inft. C.S.A.	Seattle, Washington
Joseph K. Taylor, Co. C 10th Mo. Inft. C.S.A.	Richwoods, Mo.
Wm. B. Van Nort, Co. B 4th Mo. Mtd. Inft. C.S.A.	Belleview, Mo.

Necrology

P.F. Lonergan, Captain Company D, 1st M.S.M. Inf. and Provost Marshal at Pilot Knob, Mo., in 1864, organized the Citizens' Defense Company at that place September 26, 1864. Died at San Bernardina, Cal., May 18, 1904. Was one of the Vice-Presidents of The Pilot Knob Memorial Association at the time of his demise.

Notice

Every person receiving a copy of this pamphlet is requested to forward a list of all survivors of the battle of Pilot Knob whom they may know, with their post office address, as it is desired to mail each one a copy. Extra copies of these proceedings can be had by those desiring the same, on receipt of 20 cents per copy, the money thus collected going into the monument fund of the Pilot Knob Memorial Association.

OLD FORT DAVIDSON, as it appears forty years after the Civil War; view taken from north of west looking south of east; Pilot Knob in the background at the left. This fort, which is an irregular, hexagonal redoubt, and contains slightly less than once acre of ground,

A more extended history of the battle of Pilot Knob and the first two weeks of the Price raid into Missouri in 1864, will be issued some time in 1905.

Address,
C.A. PETERSON, Cor. Secy.,
Box 980, St. Louis, Mo.

was successfully defended on September 27, 1864, by a force of 1000 Unionists under command of Gen. Thomas Ewing, Jr., against the repeated assaults of an army of 20,000 Confederates commanded by Maj.-Gen. Sterling Price.

FROM THE SECOND ANNUAL MEETING OF THE PILOT KNOB MEMORIAL ASSOCIATION ON THE FORTY-FIRST ANNIVERSARY OF THE BATTLE OF PILOT KNOB, SEPTEMBER 26TH, 27TH AND 28TH, 1905. ORIGINALLY PRINTED BY PRESS A.R. FLEMING PRINTING COMPANY, ST. LOUIS, MISSOURI.

Officers Elected for the Ensuing Year
The Pilot Knob Memorial Association

DAVID MURPHY, President, St. Louis, Mo.
H.C. WILKINSON, Secretary, Piedmont, Mo.
C.A. PETERSON, Cor. Secretary, St. Louis, Mo.
HENRY S. CARROLL, Treasurer, St. Louis, Mo.

VICE-PRESIDENTS
Wm. J. Campbell, Oakville, Iowa.
H.B. Milks, Leon, Kan.
Sam B. Rowe, Rolla, Mo.
T.M. Montgomery, Akard, Mo.
Wm. H. Smith, Park Place, Ore.
James H. Nations, Womack, Mo.
Eli D. Ake, Ironton, Mo.

ASSISTANT SECRETARIES
Hugo Hoffbauer, Buffalo, Iowa.
John A. Rice, Braswell, Mo.
James C. Steakley, Patton, Mo.
Charles Biehle, St. Louis, Mo.
James M. Travis, Greenfield, Mo.
Thos. Ewing Jr., 67 Wall St., New York, N.Y.
John S. Luthy, Pilot Knob, Mo.

Captain William J. Campbell, as he appeared in 1864, who commanded the 14th Iowa Infantry, 150 men, at the Battle of Pilot Knob and, on the retreat to Leasburg, successfully resisting repeated charges of 8,000 Confederates cavalry while falling back over twenty miles.

Summary of the Forces and Losses in the Battle of Pilot Knob

Confederate Forces

Three Divisions, composed of Nine Brigades. Made up of Thirty-three Regiments, Ten Battalions and Four Batteries, Aggregating between 25,000 and 30,000 men.

Confederate Losses

400 or more killed,
175 or more mortally wounded.
1,000 or more surviving wounded.
_____

1,575 Total.

Union Forces

Parts of Seven Regiments made up of Twenty-one Companies, or parts of Companies, and aggregating a little more than 1,000 men.

Union Losses

Killed	14
Mortally wounded	13
Surviving wounded	46
Total	73

THE PILOT KNOB MEMORIAL ASSOCIATION

The Pilot Knob Memorial Association, composed of the survivors of the battle and their friends, pursuant to a call issued by its President, David Murphy, and Secretary, H.C. Wilkinson, met in second annual reunion on the forty-first anniversary of the battle, in old Fort Davidson, at noon on September 26, 1905, and dissolved at 4:30 p.m. September 28th. The afternoon of September 26th was passed in an informal manner by survivors and visitors, reviving old acquaintance and indulging in reminiscence.

At 10:00 a.m., September 27th the Association was called to order by Col. David Murphy in business session. Thos. T. Dalton of Farmington and John S. Luthy of Pilot Knob were elected Assistant Secretaries of the meeting and reports for the past year were read including a list of participants in the battle who have died in the past year. Among those demised was Assistant Secretary John H. Delano of Murphysboro, Ill., and Comrade John S. Luthy of Pilot Knob was elected to fill the position for the ensuing year. All other officers of the Association were re-elected for the year.

Letters of regret were read from Major Wm. Warner, U.S. Senator, Congressman M.E. Rhodes and several other prominent citizens and comrades from a distance who had been invited to attend but could not be present.

A subscription was started to buy the old fort, and twenty acres surrounding it, to be preserved from desecration until the Federal government may acquire title to the same and order its preservation as a National Military Park. Several liberal donations were made toward this purpose and at 11:30 a.m. the meeting adjourned until 2:00 p.m.

At 2:00 p.m., the Association was again called to order with about 1,500 persons present and Rev. George Steele of Ironton delivered the following address of welcome:

ADDRESS OF REV. GEORGE STEELE

It has fallen to my lot this afternoon, in the absence of our Mayor, Mr. Edgar, to make the address of welcome in behalf of the citizens of Ironton, Pilot Knob and the Arcadia Valley, to the survivors of the battle of Pilot Knob in both armies, and to all visitors and friends. Now, it is always hard to be substituted on an occasion of this kind, but if you can get over your disappointment without hearing Mr. Edgar I can probably get over my embarrassment. It is always embarrassing to speak to a disappointed congregation.

I want to say, first of all, to every one of you who have come here, the survivors of this marvelous battle which took place upon this ground and near here, and to all of our visitors both young and old, we want to bid you a hearty welcome.

There are some spots on this earth which are sacred to all humanity. There are little plains between the mountains and the seas that will always have a name which will stir the blood of men as long as men live, breathe and honor patriotism.

The field of Marathon where eleven thousand brave Athenians met the hosts of Persia and drove them back to the sea will always call up memories of patriotism. It was one of the great crises of history. Go to the battlefield of Waterloo on that June afternoon ninety years ago and see on that Sunday afternoon thousands of Prussian soldiers standing on the plains there and meeting on that long hot afternoon the attacks of the French cavalry. That was also a decisive battle. Men traveled from all over the world to see that battlefield simply because it meant something to humanity, where brave men struggled and fought for what they thought to be right.

Now this is a spot I think which will always be fresh in the memory of men, because here upon this ground where we are standing was fought a battle. Insignificant it may seem to some, because in comparison with the great battles of the Civil War and compared with the numbers engaged in it, the results seemed to be insignificant, but to the latter day historian who reads between the lines, it is seen that there was fought on these grounds one of the most important battles of the Civil War. I understand that there was more blood shed on this ground here on that afternoon in September, 1864, than was shed in the battle of Santiago and the whole Cuban War. I heard some of our friends complain about the heat this afternoon but I think it was very much warmer forty-one years ago to-day than it is this afternoon, and while I haven't the least idea that the *thermometer* was any higher than it is to-day, it was very much hotter, especially to our friends who were engaged in the battle here.

I stood on the corner of this fort this morning while Col. Murphy was describing the battle to Mr. Cahoon, and I will say that I never heard a more interesting recital in my life than the one that Col. Murphy gave this morning. I bid you a most hearty welcome.

Colonel David Murphy, as he appeared in 1864, who at the Battle of Pilot Knob commanded the artillery defending Fort Davidson and wrought such havoc in the Confederate columns as to make a successful assault impossible and, by his exhibition of reckless daring, inspired the raw recruits with the courage of veterans.

ADDRESS OF COL. DAVID MURPHY

Col. David Murphy, President of the Memorial Association acknowledged the cordial welcome extended to the survivors of the battle of Pilot Knob in a few well chosen remarks, and then read the following statistics to show that the battle of Pilot Knob was not the insignificant affair which some are misled into believing it was.

Col. Murphy said: The battle of Pilot Knob deserves to be ranked among the most important and decisive battles ever fought on the American continent if we exclude the great battles of the Civil War. If that period of our country's history is to be the sole criterion in such matters, then of course, in numbers engaged and losses incurred it is not to be compared with many of the larger battles in that period.

The battles fought by Gen. Lee in the vicinity of Richmond saved that city from capture until the final collapse of the Confederacy. The battles of Antietam and Gettysburg saved Washington the Capitol as well as Philadelphia. The battle of Nashville saved Cincinnati and just as effectively the battle of Pilot Knob saved St. Louis with its vast stores of supplies of all kinds, from capture and despoliation, with a very strong claim that it did more by preventing a flank movement on the states of Illinois and Indiana, then rendered liable to invasion by the secret treasonable organizations which, at that period of time, threatened the safety of Chicago and Indianapolis. But as heretofore stated, exclude the important battles of the rebellion, so far as numbers and losses are involved, the battle of Pilot Knob ranks among the severest of any ever fought on the American continent.

The Revolutionary War

In the Revolutionary War, the first important battle fought by the colonists was Bunker Hill, the attacking force consisted of 3,000 British and the defensive force of Americans about one-half that number.

Perhaps the most decisive battle fought in that great struggle was Saratoga when the invading force under Gen. Burgoyne, amounted to 10,000 men of all arms, including Canadians and Indian allies. This force was before the battle reduced to about 7,000 men. The American force under Gen. Gates was of equal proportions, if not much larger. 5,791 men were surrendered, showing a lost of over 1,000. In the battle of Long Island, Gens. Howe and Clinton of the British army had about 11,000 men to Washington's 9,000 and that battle did not save the city of New York from capture and occupation.

At the siege of Yorktown the last of the battles of the Revolution, Gens. Washington, Lincoln, Dekalb and Von Steuben of the American force and Count Rochambeau and Lafayette of the French force, commanded 12,000 men exclusive of the Virginia militia under Gen. Nelson. The British forces under Lord Cornwallis defending the works, had a force of 7,000 men, all of whom were surrendered to the allied command.

The War of 1812

In the War of 1812–15 the largest invading British force consisted of 14,000 soldiers and sailors who were defeated by the Americans under Commodore McDonough and Gen. Macomb at Plattsburg. At New Orleans, Gen. Jackson with 6,000 sharp shooting riflemen from Kentucky and Tennessee reinforced by Lafitte's pirate artillerymen defeated 12,000 British under Gen. Pakenham.

The Mexican War

In the war with Mexico the United States government had enrolled a very large invading army amounting to 100,454 men of all arms, but when Gen. Zachary Taylor commenced his march from Camargo to Monterey where he fought for three days, Sept. 21, 22 and 23, 1846, he had an army composed of only 3,000 regulars and 3,000 volunteers. His losses in the three days' struggle amounted to 142 killed and died of wounds, and 368 wounded.

At Buena Vista, Gen. Taylor had 517 regulars and 4,400 volunteers. He fought Santa Anna for two days with a total loss of 685 killed and wounded.

At the siege of Vera Cruz, Gen. Scott had a force composed of 6,608 regulars and 6,662 volunteers, aided by the ships of the U.S. navy. The American losses were 238 killed and wounded. At Cerro Gordo, Gen. Scott's force was reduced by expiration of term of enlistment of many volunteers and he fought the Mexican army with the force of 6,000 regulars and 2,500 volunteers. His total loss in killed and wounded was 452.

At Contreras, Chapultepec and San Antonio, fought August 19 and 20, 1847, 9,691 regulars and 1,526 volunteers defeated the Mexicans, suffering a loss of 1,054. At the capture of the City of Mexico, 7,035 regulars and 1,290 volunteers were engaged on the American side and their loss was 861 killed and wounded.

The Cuban War

During the Cuban War of 1898, there was engaged a fighting force of 223,000 volunteers, to which must be added the regular establishment of say 60,000 men, but only 24,000 of these were actually on the field of operations. The total losses in that campaign amounted to 289 killed and wounded.

The battle of Pilot Knob was fought Sept. 27, 1864, between the invading force commanded by Gen. Sterling Price with 24,000 Confederates on one side and the force defending the earthwork called Fort Davidson, on which we now are gathered, and the rifle pits radiating therefrom, amounted to 1,000 men of all arms commanded by Gen. Thomas Ewing and Col. Thos. C. Fletcher.

Three desperate assaults were made by the two divisions commanded by Maj. Gens. J.S. Marmaduke and Fagan, consisting of well-seasoned and experienced troops, and they were defeated and repulsed and driven back to Arcadia a distance of two miles, after which the Union forces under Gen. Ewing made a successful retreat to Leasburg, a distance of 65 miles where another stand was made and every preparation for another sanguinary conflict.

But when Gen. Price's forces reinforced by Gen. Jo Shelby's division arrived in front of Leasburg in pursuit and saw the earthworks constructed during the night by Gen. Ewing's men, they refused to deliver an assault for the reason stated by Gen. Price in his report of the campaign dated at Washington, Ark., Dec. 28, 1864: "The enemy having thrown up fortifications during the night it was deemed advisable not to renew the attack and the forces were withdrawn." Gen. Shelby in his report also made in December, 1864, giving an excuse for not making a further demonstration against Gen. Ewing's little force said, "The enemy spent their time in throwing up heavy fortifications and it was considered best next morning not to renew the attack," and this formidable invading army which entered Missouri with high sounding purposes marched away to the west, away from St. Louis, its original point to be taken, leaving Gen. Ewing's devoted little band in full possession of their works where they remained until ordered away to Rolla.

Compare any battle in ancient or modern history and where is there an instance in which so small a force as Ewing's successfully "held the fort" against so formidable an assault? I venture to say that no such instance can be found.

The nearest approach to it occurred B.C. 490 when 110,000 Persians attacked 11,000 Athenians and Plataeans under Miltiades on the plains of

Marathon. The Persans [*sic*] were repulsed and driven to their ships with which they sought to reach Athens before Miltiades could intercept them, but in this they were foiled. Miltiades retired from Marathon, took position near Athens, and when the Persians saw the travel-stained, bleeding warriors who had so fiercely routed them, they refused to attack, and withdrew with their ships leaving Athens saved by the devotion and bravery of its heroic defenders. What the battle of Marathon was to Athens, the battle of Pilot Knob was to St. Louis.

ADDRESS BY HON. B.B. [BENJAMIN BENSON] CAHOON

Mr. President, comrades, ladies and gentlemen: Someone has said that:
"A pebble in the streamlet scant,
Has changed the course of many a river,
A dewdrop on the baby plant
Has warped the giant oak forever."

Whether that be true or not I do not know, but this is true: Every student of history has remarked that important events are founded often on apparently insignificant circumstances. It is my good fortune to-day to tell my old friend, Col. Murphy, and the other comrades who survived and are here, who participated in the battle of Pilot Knob on September 27, 1864, something they have never before heard, namely the truthful origin of that battle. It occurred thiswise [*sic*]. On the 24th of September, 1864, pursuant to orders given in Arkansas and elsewhere, the entire three divisions of Gen. Price's army concentrated at Fredericktown, 22 miles east of this place, and where I reside. The last of the stragglers had assembled there by nightfall and the General took up his headquarters on the summit of the hill whereon my home now stands and spent the night of the 24th there, expecting, after a little rest, on the morning of the 25th to continue the march as contemplated by him to St. Louis. He expected its easy capture. They were all there on all sides of the hill and in the creek bottom on the east and in the meadow on the west side of what is now my home. They were supremely confident that by forced marches, in three or four days St. Louis would be theirs. On the morning of the 25th of September there appeared at Gen. Price's headquarters a youth by the name of Alexander Nifong, or "Little Alec" as he was called, and with that independence which characterizes a 12-year old boy he confidently but politely advanced to the General and said (as he years afterwards repeated the story to me): "Gen. Price, I want your permission to go through your army to find my father's mules, for your soldiers must have them." The mules had strayed outside of his father's home property nearby and the youth concluded that the mules must be there. The General said to him: "My lad, you are out of place; you should go to the Yankee camp to find your mules." "No, General, my mules are not in the Yankee camp, for I left the Yankee camp at Pilot Knob this morning at daybreak and my mules were not there." The General said, "Who are you?" The boy said, "I told you my name was Alec Nifong." "Well," said the General, "Are you a Southern boy or a Yankee lad?" The boy said, "Everybody knows that every Nifong in this county is a rebel." "Well," said the General, "I would like to have some one vouch for the truthfulness of this statement[.]" "They will," said the lad, "right down there in that little concrete house is my old grandfather, Uncle George Nifong, as we call him." "Oh, yes," said the General, "he has been up here with a number of other Nifongs to pay their respects to me, but my lad, I want to know that you are a Nifong so I will send for your grandfather to see if he will vouch for you[.]" The venerable George Nifong was accordingly sent for and soon came up there. Then General Price said to him: "Do you know this lad?" "Yes, General, I do; that's my grandson Alec." "Do you know where he has been for the last day or so?" "Yes, I understand that Alec has been out looking for his father's pair of stray mules." "Now," said the General, "my boy you can continue your story and be sure to tell me the truth in answer to every question that I ask you. When did you go to Pilot Knob?" "I went there yesterday morning." That would be the 24th of September, 1864. "Who did you see there?" "I saw a lot of our home guard militia up there and a lot of our boys from this county and Dent County and Wayne County, but they do not amount to anything for they are a gang of cowardly home guards." "Do you remember the names of any of the officers you saw up there?" "Yes, I saw Major Wilson and a man by the name of Major Dave Murphy and all those small fry fellows who command these cowardly home guards." "Well, my lad, how many guns did you see?" "I saw thirteen cannon there." The General smilingly shook his head and said: "That's an unlucky number of guns for them Yankees." That was his first expression. "How many soldiers were there in all," the General asked the boy. "General Price," said the boy, "I saw General Carlin's troops march through Fredericktown to participate in the battle here in 1861 and there's not one-third as many Yankee soldiers up there as there were Yankee soldiers at the battle of Fredericktown." And there on the sides of the hill and all around him the boy saw Confederate artillery and cavalry to the number of over twenty thousand. "Why, Gen. Price," said the boy, "all the Yankees up there would not be a flea bite to all these men you've got."

General Price soliloquized to himself, and then said, "I believe the boy is right." Turning to his Adjutant-General, he said, "Give the orders that Shelby's division shall, by forced marches, proceed at once and get between Pilot Knob and St. Louis, somewhere about Mineral Point, and give the further orders that the whole of the balance of my command shall immediately proceed to march to Pilot Knob. It is one day's longer march to St. Louis and we will capture that garrison there at a loss of not exceeding more than a day and a half, and as St. Louis is the objective point, the capture of that garrison and its guns will so terrify these Yankee soldiers in St. Louis that we will have but very little trouble in gobbling it and them up, that being the great purpose of our invasion of Missouri."*

And so, comrades, ladies and gentlemen, that was the origin of the battle of Pilot Knob. Those troops left Fredericktown after an early dinner on the 25th, and strange and miraculous as it may seem, General Ewing likewise started from St. Louis to take command at Pilot Knob about the same hour, as I understand it, that Price started with his army from Fredericktown to gobble up this little army of "cowardly home guards" with their unfortunate thirteen guns. Well, you know that the battle of Pilot Knob cut deeply into the consequences of the history of our Civil War. There was no other battle like it in the whole history of our country and practically none in the history of the world. I was then in the army of the Potomac, and we were fighting with Grant and Lee as commanders fairly even battles as to numbers, but at

---

General Price, in his official report of the raid, says: "I received at Fredericktown satisfactory information that the strength of the enemy at Ironton was about 1,500 and that the Federal General, A.J. Smith, was encamped about ten miles from St. Louis with his corps, composed of about 8,000 infantry, on the St. Louis and Iron Mountain Railroad. I immediately issued orders to Brig. Gen'l Shelby to proceed at once with his division by the way of Farmington to a point on the St. Louis and Iron Mountain Railroad where there were three fine bridges in close proximity to each other, and to destroy the railroad there and the bridges; after accomplishing that object to fall back in the direction of Ironton and Pilot Knob, which would effectually prevent Gen'l A.J. Smith from re-enforcing the garrison at those places, while I would attack and take them with the divisions of Major Generals Fagan and Marmaduke."

the battle of Pilot Knob one thousand Union soldiers resisted and defeated over sixteen thousand Confederates: killed and wounded of them 1575, while their total loss in killed and wounded was about 73. Therefore, I say that for its results that the Union victory here in all probability saved St. Louis from capture. Considering the few Union soldiers here and the vastly superior numbers of Confederates, but one thousand Union soldiers arrayed against at least sixteen thousand Confederates (for Price had 24,000 men and Shelby's division which immediately started for Mineral Point left him at least 14,000 or 16,000 men to gobble up that "worthless little garrison"). Considering the result the battle is historic. They came, as you all know, reaching here on the morning of the 26th, as Col. Murphy so graphically describes in that magnificent speech made here a year ago, a speech worthy to be declared the official history and true account of the Union forces at and the details of the battle of Pilot Knob. The pickets were driven in, but it is no slight matter, fellow citizens, as we old soldiers know, to march an army twenty-two miles with its cannon, ammunition and commissary stores and to prepare it for battle. And although the Confederates got here on the 26th to drive in our pickets on that day, yet Price was not ready to open that battle until the 27th, and you all know how it was done. The heroism on the picket line was prophetic of what was to come. You deceived and misled General Price so much by the courage of your pickets on yonder (Pilot Knob) mountain and in that (Arcadia) valley, that he concluded that soldiers who were making such stout resistance on the picket line must be handsomely and well supported by a great reserve force. But at last about this hour (2:30 p.m.) or a little before as you have been told before, and the story never grows old, for heartache days and circumstances of the Civil War never will grow old, the battle of Pilot Knob began. In the lapse of time, this too-much forgotten battle will loom up as the most magnificent small battle that was fought in American history. I want to tell you a little story in connection with that battle. You know how Col. Murphy delayed to open the action. He said, "Let them open first so that they cannot say that I took advantage of them," and they did fire their guns first. An old rebel soldier who is at Fredericktown said that he was in the battery on the Confederate side, and that he fired the first shot. I asked him who fired the second shot, he said that "some Yankee fired the second shot and knocked his gun endways." That Confederate battery was soon silenced, and then they came on, column after column, a solid mass of soldiers, against and to wipe out this little band of "cowardly home guards" and those supposed insignificant Iowa men and the gunners who were behind those unfortunate thirteen guns. And how did it all result? You all know. In victory for our little band, every man of whom was a hero.

Fellow citizens, what was the inspiration of that battle? The Union soldiers knew not each other. They had been assembled here too quickly to get acquainted with each other. Gen. Thos. Ewing, Jr., their commander, got in this fort on the day before the battle. Col. Murphy had been here but a little while before. They had no personal acquaintance with each other; on the other hand they were all comparative strangers to each other. "The cowardly home guards" had never before fired a shot at a greater enemy than squirrel, deer or wild turkey. But thank God they were fine shots, although every man of them practically was a backwoods boy. So that was the first apparent discordant element. The next was the great disparity of numbers; more than ten trained Confederates to attack one Union soldier who was not a veteran. Imagine, ladies and gentlemen, what would be our sensations if all of us who are on these grounds to-day, men and women (and they exceed the number of Union soldiers here on that memorable 27th day of September, 1864, at this hour); imagine what would be our sensations if we were posted on yonder angle of this fort with even good, modern, repeating rifles in our hands, as were not the kind the old boys had on that day, for they did not have repeating guns, and they had the old ram rod smooth bore muskets, what would be our sensations if we saw coming down that valley in solid columns over twelve thousand men, all in battle array, with their rifles at right shoulder shift, with their bayonets fixed and all glistening in the sunlight, advancing to make short work of that insolent Yankee garrison of "cowardly home guards" and good-for-nothing Iowa soldiers and their unfortunate thirteen guns. What would be our sensations, knowing that they meant death, knowing that they meant destruction; what would be our sensations if they were approaching us to-day? I know not what would be our sensations, but I know what transpired over there on that rampart. One of the soldiers standing upon it was a youth, a young miner from Mine LaMotte. He had not even had the advantage of farm and backwoods training. He had never been even a country school-teacher, nor could he shoot a running deer behind its front quarters. He had been accustomed to mining lead, working under ground all his life. He has told me of the impressions that he gathered as Gen. Price's large army marched on this historic fort. Said he: "There I was trembling and wishing I was at home, for those rebels came in their terrible array and I felt that death was certainly our fate, when suddenly Col. Murphy coolly got up and walked on the rampart." There then as you know were Confederates on every side, coming down yonder sloping mountain side, and massed in front of this fort all in solid array. They were sufficient to terrify a veteran much less a little German miner who had worked underground all his life. He said that Col. Murphy arose on that rampart and he moved seriously, calmly, quietly, determinedly. As he walked he would look at the Union soldiers then inside the ramparts, and his look imparted to them what he meant that it should, courage, courage, courage to do their duty! As the Confederates approached, the Colonel sang out: "Come on, come on, and hurry up! Come close enough so that we can see the whites of your eyes." The German said that when he saw that sight all his fear left him, his tremors ceased shaking his frame, and he felt that if that man could do that and not be shot down in an instant he could at least stand up and fight. Fortunately in every great epoch of our great history, when the occasion arose for him the needed man arose. It was so as to Washington in our Revolutionary struggle, it was so as to Grant in our Civil War and it was so as to David Murphy at the battle of Pilot Knob. Col. Murphy did something he did not have time to analyze, but if he had analyzed and been poetical he would have said:

"Enough, if something in my hand have power,
To live and move and shape the future hour,
And if toward the silent tomb we go,
Through Faith, through Hope, and Love's transcendent dower,
We feel that we are greater than we know."

It was the inspiration in Col. Murphy to seize the need and be equal to the circumstances of that fateful hour. He felt that if his life had then to go out to encourage his comrades, well let it go! Thank God it did not go. And thank God that he and many other old comrades are spared to meet us to-day here, on this occasion. Thank God also comrades, that it was not your fate, as it was the fate of poor Tesreau and others of the fourteen heroes who here fell bleeding and soon lay silent in the embrace of death on that memorable day to find their last resting places on the field of that battle. Their inanimate bodies were deposited on the top of the fort magazine and finally when our troops were retiring, the magazine was exploded and these men found their historic graves beneath the blown debris of that magazine and they are sleeping there now at our feet. Uncover! Kneel to them! Oh, never let this field, this old fort, comrades, get out of our hands. This is sacred ground. It has been consecrated by holy blood spent in the holiest cause for which men ever died. There lie our dead comrades in that depression! That they so lie is all the more reason this fort should belong to you, belong to the Nation. Let us say to each other it shall not get out of our own and the Nation's hands. Let us raise money and buy the sacred spot of land and apply to our Government to take it off our hands and improve it and commemorate it forever for what it is; an heroic and historic battle ground. I can scarcely realize nor can you that forty-one years have elapsed since that memorable day. How different the scene! Then at this hour the cannon were booming. Then the waspish Minnie ball was striking these banks and wounding and killing our comrades, and then peal on peal from your cannon was mowing lines and lines in the advancing Confederate charge. Then the rattle of your musketry was adding further destruction to your cannon. Then when you saw the Confederates waver and you saw them give way, retreat and scatter, you continued to fire your cannon and your muskets all the more rapidly because they were on the retreat and you scarcely ceased to do both until they were two miles away from "them cowardly home guards" and "them worthless, good-for-nothing Iowa soldiers" and their miserable thirteen cannon. Then it was that the inspiration of victory filled your souls. We can scarcely realize it all. Imagination easily brings again to your vision the old scene, but how changed all now is! Even this fort is not the same as it was forty-one years ago to-day. These trees have grown up in it as others have grown over the other battle fields of the rebellion. Birds are building their nests in the mouths of deserted cannon, and our comrades sleep as they so long have slept their long, long sleep. Thank God it is not the sleep of forgetfulness! As we recall our resting comrades on this and on every other battlefield of the Civil War we can say: "Rest, comrades, rest, and sleep. No longer does the alarm of battle disturb you; no longer is your repose disturbed. Here there is for you the truce of God." They do not hear our eulogisms, but comrades, all mankind to-day are speaking their eulogisms and it will only be a little while until the remnant of us left will pass away, but comrades, their fame and your fame will never die. That Civil War was founded on the spirit of the Declaration of Independence, which declared that all men were free and entitled to equal rights and liberty and to the pursuit of happiness. We had to fight out the inevitable battle of slavery on the one hand and liberty on the other, and in spite of the shifts and compromises to avoid that war, slavery perished in blood and the result of the war was liberty for all men for all time. Those of us who enlisted were fighting for something higher and sublimer than the geographical union of the United States of America. We were fighting the battle of human freedom the world over. The United States by remaining a united nation whose genius is liberty regulated by law, has become the greatest power, the greatest intellectually and the greatest liberty-loving nation in the world, whose influence is moulding all governments after the spirit of our own. But how did it become so? Abraham Lincoln was our hero and when we speak the name of Abraham Lincoln how memory comes back to us. How we remember his homely and ungainly figure, his great charity, patience and his great love of the common people and his saving common sense. How we remember how he tried to interpret the wish and will and keep close to the people in sentiment, hoping that they would ultimately reach the position that he desired, that of universal liberty for mankind. Now, the point is this, and remember this and transmit it to your children, that all we have to-day, our united great country and all it stands for to-day are owing to two circumstances. Lincoln was our leader, and as such he only upheld the flag. You the rank and file of the union army who bore on your shoulders your muskets and upheld by your bayonets the life and the hope of this nation, you are the heroes of the Civil War. You all remember how everything was dark and black and gloomy at the outset and how they had all the southern national forts. We who survived remember the time when we heard that the flag was fired upon at Fort Sumpter. Each man as to that event had his own emotions and each survivor has his own story. I recall that it was on a Saturday afternoon and my father came home and I, a farmer lad but fifteen years old was watering at the old well the stock, but had been reading the papers, said: "Father, I hear that they have fired on Fort Sumpter, is it true?" "Yes," said my father, "and you will scarcely live to see the end of this effort to divide and destroy our government unless the people of this country arise and avenge the insult to our country's flag and maintain the unity, dignity and integrity of this nation.'" I remember how the words burned into my soul and I thought of the beauty of the flag, thought of all it had in the past meant for all: peace, home, country and national glory. As a school boy I learned to recite a little poetry and I repeated the lines to myself as I thought of our beautiful banner being fired upon, that flag which meant our united country which our fathers had established for us and how wicked it was to fire on that flag or drag it in the dust and seek to destroy the then only free government of the people on earth. My boyhood poetical soul repeated then as I repeat now the inspiration:

> "Invincible Banner! Flag of the Free!
> O, where is the foot that would falter for Thee?
> Or the arms that would be folded till triumph is won,

And the Eagle looks proud as of old to the Sun.
Give tears to the parting; a murmur of prayer,
Then forward, the fame of our standard to share,
With a welcome to wounding and battle and scars,
And the glory of death for the Stripes and the Stars."

And we all likewise animated rallied around that flag. We left the plow in the furrow and soon we were drilling in camps, to prepare for actual war and for four long years, through 625 battlefields and skirmishes, we bore that flag until at last it triumphed supreme. You all know what has been the subsequent results. All the Confederates I know have realized and rejoiced in the fact that this is not a broken nation, whose desire for world place disarms warring nations, but is one united nation, and I am glad that they realize that it is better that we should have a united nation than sundry belligerent and discordant peoples. The United States is now the arbiter of the destiny of the world; is controller of its peace, simply because the rank and file of the Union army from 1861 to 1865, loved, stood by and fought to preserve for us and mankind our country. I think that the harmonizing spirit commenced at Appomattox. When Gen. Lee surrendered the rebel soldiers were without food, and you know that a man cannot fight long on an empty stomach. It fell to the lot of us boys, Grant's seasoned veterans who had five days' rations in our haversacks, to begin to fraternize with those starved, ragged rebels, and it fell to my lot to care for two Alabama Confederate soldiers. The first thing I did was to give them some hardtack. Though it was good and hard, they ravenously ate it. I then gave them some fried bacon and a quart each of coffee. Up to the coffee those two old rebels were silent, morose, sullen and stubborn. When the coffee arrived they were a little complacent, and when they smoked my pipe they were a little more so. I said to one of the rebels: "That was good coffee, reb." One rebel said to me, "Yank, all coffee like this is good coffee." I said, "If you boys will come into the Union and behave yourselves you can have coffee like that the balance of your days. The other rebel said, "I have about made up my mind to do that very thing, but I tell you Yank, if we'd had coffee like that, we could have licked all you Yanks with clubs."

It was written in the book of fate by the inscrutable finger of God that this government was to live and continue its high, holy and supreme mission and that our descendants and mankind were to honor and love the heroes of Gettysburg, Chickamauga and Pilot Knob, and the other battles of the war. God bless you comrades. May we often meet here again.

Speech of Gen. C.W. Pavey

Comrades and fellow citizens: I am astonished; more so I presume than any of you can possibly be. I have traveled very nearly all over the United States, sailed the Pacific Ocean and the Atlantic Ocean, and fished in the lakes of the north and the Gulf of Mexico. I have rowed up and down the streams that still bind the North and South together. I have been in almost every state in the Union, but I swear I never was in Ironton before.

With my distinguished friend and your distinguished fellow citizen, Col. Pat Dyer, and some other gentlemen, I came here to look on and hear them say something, but now they have by some means or other taken advantage of me and asked me to help them. Now, comrades, we must not forget the advice of the distinguished gentleman (Mr. Cahoon) whom I had the pleasure to hear address you before me for a few moments; purchase this ground, oh, yes. If you cannot raise the money, come over in Egypt and I will dig out and raise a few dollars. I would go further. I would go down here to Emerson Park and buy every foot of it. And that old oak tree too. I live in the state thank God that brought to light General Grant. I live in grand old imperial Illinois, the state that gave us Abraham Lincoln, the greatest man born since the birth of the world's Saviour, and if you cannot raise enough money to purchase this ground, come over to Illinois and we will help you do it. I have a supreme respect for any man who will stand up and fight and who faces the cannon and shot, and who braved the rebel forts for his flag. He is entitled to everything good and sweet in this country and to have passes over every railroad so that he could go wherever he wanted to go, and a pension for himself, and one for his wife, and schooling for his children and everything on earth that is good in this United States, for without his effort we would not have had a government. We would have had a government of states. I could not then have come from Illinois into Missouri without permission from old Price or someone else in Missouri. We fought for the United States and the flag. It has been said that we fought to free the negroes. I thank God Almighty that they are free to-day in this United States, but it was to save the Union that we fought. I was in Alabama a few days ago, and a gentleman said to me, "I see you were in the war." I said, "Yes." "You went clear through it?" "Yes." "Were you in favor of your government in every move that they made?" "Yes." "Were you in favor of arming the negroes?" "Yes, I would arm a jackass if he would kick you." If I were a minister I would put the flag up over the pulpit and nothing save the cross of the world's Redeemer should go above it. Then I would say, "Come up all you sinners and get religion, seek it under the flag, and those of you who won't come under the flag may go to the devil so far as I care, but you must come under the flag." There is no place too sacred on this earth for the Stars and Stripes to wave. Now she waves so high that every nation on the globe can see it. The country was saved and we rejoice to-day over a restored union. The prophetic words which the gentleman referred to to-day have been fulfilled and to-day we are united in sounding the praises of the Union in every state of the Union. I want to put the flag on every school house, and thanks to some women in our state she waves on every schoolhouse in Illinois. God bless the patriotic women, the wives and sweethearts and mothers of the heroes of this country. Some of those heroes lie buried here to-day; this ground should be kept sacred forever and ever. Put the flag over it and keep it there. Let the Grand Army take it up and go down in their pockets and see that this sacred ground, all of it, is purchased. Let this be a place where the hundred and thousands may come and pay the respects to the memories of such men as General Grant and the heroes of this battle.

Address by Col. D.P. Dyer

I came down here to-day to pay my respects to Col. Murphy and those who were associated with him in this place forty-one years ago to-day. I have lived in Missouri for more than sixty years, but I have never had the pleasure before of coming to see this ground. I want to emphasize by what I say now of the deep obligation the people of this country are under to Col. Murphy and those who were with him forty-one years ago.

I was connected with the army to some extent myself, and while you were engaged here at this place, I was engaged elsewhere in Missouri. While the battle of Pilot Knob was being fought, war was rampant all over the state. On the day that you fought here, in North Missouri men were put to as severe a test as in any place in the United States.

On the 28th day of September, 1864, the day after this gallant fight was made here, it was my unpleasant duty to be in command of the troops that took up the bodies of our unfortunate comrades who were massacred at Centralia, in Boone County, Mo., the day before, my regiment being on its way to Jefferson City to resist the impending attack there. As you were resisting the onslaught here, a force under the command of General Clinton B. Fisk, whom many of you knew, was assembled at Jefferson City to resist the coming into the capitol of General Price and his army. The reason why an assault was never made upon the capitol of the state by General Price's army at that time, was because of the resistance that had been made to his army at Pilot Knob. Your men here were the first to deliver a blow at the army that invaded the state in September, 1864, and it was that terrific resistance which you delivered here that saved other portions of the state from being assailed by that army. In numbers, so far as the Federal force was concerned, they were insignificant but nowhere in the history of that great strife was more courage displayed than was displayed by the little garrison when assailed by twenty times their number in this valley, the Arcadia. These men that stood here at that time delivered a blow to the invading army that did as much to save Missouri as any other blow that was ever struck in this state. Now I am not here to recount to you all of the bitter feelings that were engendered among our people at that time; I am here to-day as a citizen of Missouri to congratulate you, and all of our fellow citizens, upon the splendid condition of Missouri to-day. I came here to thank you for the services which you rendered, and I came here to thank the brave men against whom you fought for thus cheerfully upholding the flag which you upheld then. The time has past for bitter animosities. We will revere and keep sacred in our hearts the memory of those men who struggle to uphold the American flag, but our thoughts are turned to the rising sun and we are standing by each other, shoulder to shoulder, all over this country in upholding the dignity and glory of the American Republic. You and I have lived to see the time when the bitter animosities which were engendered at that time have died out, and the old gray headed men who served in both armies are keeping step to the music of the Union. They were working elbow to elbow in upholding the dignity and honor of this Republic. You have seen in your lifetimes, boys sprung from Union soldiers and boys sprung from Confederate soldiers lifting up together the flag of the American nation and fighting for it, and dying for it upon foreign lands and upon foreign seas. Bring together the people of this nation and let us learn to know each other, because no man of this country who ever faced an American did not know that he was facing a soldier and the blood of his own blood, and the flesh of his own flesh. Why, we in Missouri know something of that. I was born in the old state of Virginia; my father came to Missouri in 1841; I was the youngest of twelve children; not a single brother shared with me the views that I shared; they went to the Confederate army; they were as honest as I was honest and they were braver, possibly, than I; they were wrong as I maintain, and I was right, but they were sincere, they were honest and fought bravely for what they believed to be right. As last peace came to bless this land; the old flag was put back on every pole from which it was taken; and to-day there is good will and harmony among all the people of this country; let no foreign foe offend that flag for the men whom you battled with forty years ago will stand close by you now to resent that insult as you would resent it yourself. I tell you that when we come to compare what we are and what we would have been but for this result, there is no difference of opinion. You and I applaud our officers, they applaud theirs, and I would not deprive one of them of the privilege of honoring the men that led them in battle, although we differed with them. But thank God, to-day in this land, we are a united people and our people are standing together shoulder to shoulder forever. You and I have seen this country prosper and grow in strength almost beyond comparison. When I first came to this state it did not have a mile of railroad in its borders, but I have lived to see more than 6,000 miles of railroad built and put in operation within its limits. I have seen every portion of this great commonwealth brought together, where enterprise, energy and push has had sway. You have built churches and schoolhouses; you have built up the waste places and the houses that were burned during the Civil War leaving only a blackened chimney to mark the spot, have been replaced by other and better houses, and while we are blest with prosperity let us always be willing to do what is right, and never do what is wrong. Let us be just to every man and nation, demanding nothing for ourselves but that which is right, and yielding nothing which is wrong to any people on the face of the earth. We have been blest as no people in this world have been blest before by the gift of good men in high public offices, and never since Washington sat in the president's chair has any man occupied it against whose personal integrity aught could be said. I say this as an American citizen; whether he has been Democrat or Republican, no man has ever attacked the personal character or integrity of the ruler of this country of ours.

Something has been said about the men who died here. My friend Col. Murphy has said that I was from Pike County; that is true. I have lived in St. Louis for thirty years, but I do not believe that any man in Missouri ever credited me with being a citizen of St. Louis. They always say, "He came from Pike County." And I did. Now, may I not stand here before you and say that I am proud to be here to voice for a moment the respect of the people of Pike County for the men who fought here? Here upon this battlefield stood as brave a man from Pike County as ever drew a blade in any war in the world and that was Robert McElroy. There was old Col. Lonergan, who was true and faithful to every duty of citizenship of this country. A gentleman has handed me a list of men from Pike County who were here in the battle who were officers of the line. This is the list: Capt. Robert McElroy, Capt. Abjhah Johns, Capt. John W. Hendrick, Capt. Hiram A. Rice, Capt. P.F. Lonergan, Capt. Hugh M. Bradley, Lieut. Henry Sladek, Lieut. Jas. A Blain and Lieut. Warren C. Shattuck.

Of these officers of Missouri regiments who fought with you here at that time only two survive to-day, and they are Capt. John W. Hendrick and Lieut. Warren C. Shattuck. These men were here from my old county of Pike and Major James Wilson from the adjoining county of Lincoln, where the bodies of my father and mother are in ashes to-day. I know to be true all that Col. Murphy has said of the gallantry of Major Wilson. He was as brave a knight as ever lived and bled and as true a man as ever delivered battle. He went to his death and with him went the boys of Pike County and Lincoln County.

I came here more at the instance of the officers of your Association, who said that "you ought to go down there even if your court is in session; you ought to go down to Pilot Knob and there speak for such men as Lonergan, Johns and McElroy and that class of men that rendered service here forty-one years ago,["] and I am glad to be with you.

Say what you please about locality, you men who were born and raised here in the shade of these mountains that surround this beautiful valley, there is no place so beautiful to you as are the shades of this mountain in this great valley. So it is to every man who lives here and loves the place of his birth. I love the old county of Pike and the county of Lincoln, because in those counties I lived all my younger manhood days, and whenever one of the citizens of those counties has planted a standard that led in the right direction to civilization and good government, I have always been proud of that man.

Now, I have been over this railroad a good many times, as I have also canvassed the state, generally, but never have I stopped between Bismarck on one side of you here and Poplar Bluff on the other to make political speeches. But I know you people. Many of you here in Iron County came from old sturdy stock and many of you are newcomers. The old settlers of this county came here from old Virginia, Kentucky, North Carolina and New England, as sturdy and virtuous a people as ever forefathered a commonwealth. But talking about your own country and the people you came from, I love every stump in the blue mountain state of old Virginia. It was there I was born. But be true to your entire country. Learn to be liberal one to the other. Forget all prejudices and lookout for the coming; the past is beneath you. We cannot uncover the remains of these brave men here to-day. We can preserve them and we can keep them and we will keep them, but let us look to the glory of the entire country and to the good of every citizen. Let men grow bigger as they grow older; let them forgive as they expect to be forgiven. I want to see these things come. Thos. C. Fletcher, the Governor elected in November, 1864, sleeps at St. Louis in a beautiful cemetery, a man that probably incurred as much criticism among those who differed with him politically as any man in Missouri, because of the time that then existed. Let us all remember Fletcher, revere the sacrifices that he made and the good that he did in this state, and let no man be mean enough to undertake to dive into his grave for the purpose of offending such a man as he. You make nothing by that, but you only get the criticisms of those who believe in nobler things. Let us stand for our country and for law and order. Let it be so that every man in this country must obey the law; no man is higher than the law, and when one violates it punish the man for violating the law. This is a government by law and the man who undertakes to set up his own judgment against the law, must be taught to obey the law. Stand by the law; stand by our fathers; be good citizens of the State of Missouri. Send your children to school and teach them to love the constitution and obey the law; teach them to honor the American flag, for it makes better citizens of them, makes peace in their neighborhood and peace in the community.

Something has been said of the women of this country. The men fought during the war and were brave fellows and some of you wear badges of honor for your part in that strife. But no soldier that ever fought deserves more honor than the wife who took care of his children at home while he was gone to the army. They were the bravest. When you started with your musket on your shoulder, with the fife and drum beating, and your flag flying, you gladly went off with your comrades, but there stood watching in the window your wife with your children in her arms, who during your absence had to battle for a living. No man was ever as brave or made as many sacrifices as did the women. Let all men do honor to our brave women and teach your boys to honor the girls. Lift up your community, lift up your children and lift up your neighbor's children. No good man ever went along the street and saw his neighbor's children in trouble, that he did not symathize [sic] and speak a word of comfort to them. You do not know how much good you are doing by speaking a kind word to a boy whose whole life may be turned, as a stream is often turned by dropping in a little pebble. I have said more than I intended on coming here, but I have availed myself of impressing upon you the importance of good citizenship and to see that the boys and girls are brought up in the right direction. Do your duty. Make a park here that will be an honor to your county and community, and let the flag fly from sunrise to sunset so that it will be an inspiration to your children to give their services as you gave yours.

Address of Henry Fairback, Department Commander, G.A.R.

Mr. President: I thank you for the honor conferred upon me as the representative of the Grand Army of the Republic, by an invitation to speak on this beautiful autumn day, where, forty-one years ago, a great battle was fought. To-day all is peace in the Union, which the comrades of our splendid order so loyally and patriotically maintained and preserved, and we are now here as brothers to help celebrate the fiery contest, where two score years ago those who opposed us fought to dismantle our Union of States, the greatest, most humane government ever created by the ablest and most liberty loving patriots, who gave us the Declaration of Independence, our Constitution and brought forth after a seven years' war a nation, ruled by the people, of the people and for the people. Every bullet and pound of powder fired at this fort and the Union soldiers, clarified and purified the polluted political atmosphere which for fifty years caused the crises which culminated in the unfortunate Civil War. We were boys when we enlisted and our now wrinkled brows were then fair; our eyes were not dimmed in their vision; the frost that never melts had not gathered in our hair, and our steps were strong and active in their precision. The years have wrought their furrows in every comrade's brow, old age makes their once firey [*sic*] limbs quake and there is less laughter and song, for we can no more double-quick. They are slowly but surely crossing to the golden shores over the river.

Yet this terrible contest of battle, sword and fire, brought forth the mighty, latent strength of the American Republic's manhood. We have had and ever will have a higher respect for America's laws, its flag and its institutions by the testing of the united dormant strength of this great county, which before the war was held up and ridiculed by the press, pulpit and the political forum in Congress and the state legislatures also. That this four years' contest has after all been a blessing to the nation unforseen [*sic*] is beyond question, if our Republic, its leaders and political statesmen are recognized as the leaders and arbiters of peace, fairness and honesty, as between the nations of the world. I thank you Mr. President and may the blessings of the Almighty be with you one and all so as to be happy and contented.

On the evening of September 27th a camp fire was held in the old Fort Davidson under the auspices of U.S. Grant Post 579 G.A.R. of Pilot Knob, at which a large assembly of survivors of the battle and visiting comrades gathered and fraternized until a late hour.

On September 28th survivors and visiting comrades reviewed the battlefield and compared notes and recollections on the battle and at 4:30 p.m. the meeting informally dissolved.

Survivors Present

The following survivors of the battle of Pilot Knob were present at the second annual reunion of The Pilot Knob Memorial Association, September 26th to 28th, 1905.

H.H. Ashbaugh, Co. A, 3rd M.S.M. Cav., Starkdale, Mo.
Wm. Bell, Co. E, 47th Mo. Inf., Howes Mill, Mo.
J.L. Bennett, Co. G, 47th Mo. Inf., Piedmont, Mo.
Jefferson Bess, Co. K, 3rd M.S.M. Cav., Lutesville, Mo.
H.C. Bonney, Co. L, 3rd M.S.M. Cav., Lesterville, Mo.
David Borders, Co. E, 47th Mo. Inf., Zalma, Mo.
Isaac M. Bounds, Co. G, 47th Mo. Inf., Greenville, Mo.
Wm. J. Campbell, Capt. Commanding 14th Ia. Inf., Oakville, Ia.
C.C. Chandler, Co. F, 47th Mo. Inf., Bonne Terre, Mo.
Willis Cole, citizen defender, Ironton, Mo.
H.Q. Collins, Co. K, 3rd M.S.M. Cav., Dongola, Mo.
I.H. Crews, Col. L, 2nd M.S.M. Cav., Puxico, Mo.
Thos. T. Dalton, Com. Dept., Farmginton, Mo.
B.C. Davidson, Co. E, 5th Mo. Inf., Caledonia, Mo.
Thos. L. Davidson, Co. C, 14th Ia. Inf., Searsboro, Ia.
Herman Davis, citizen defender, Ironton, Mo.
Isaac H. Dillon, Co. D, 3rd M.S.M. Cav., Marling, Mo.
John W. Evans, Co. A, 47th Mo. Inf., Lodi, Mo.
Geo. W. Farrar, citizen surgeon, Ironton, Mo.
Wm. A. Fletcher, Co. E, 47th Mo. Inf., Arcadia, Mo.
Thos. Fortune, Co. E, 50th Mo. Inf., Caledonia, Mo.
Henry Fry, Co. H, 3rd M.S.M. Cav., Doe Run, Mo.
Henry Gaines, Co. K, 3rd M.S.M. Cav., Zalma, Mo.
W.T. Gay, citizen defender, Ironton, Mo.

S.A. Harris, Sergt. Co. A, 47th Mo. Inf., Patterson, Mo.

Ephraim Hasty, Co. K, 3rd M.S.M. Cav., Fredericktown, Mo.

W.W. Haywood, citizen defender, Ironton, Mo.

E.K. Hopkins, Co. F, 47th Mo. Inf., Farmington, Mo.

Frederick Kaths, citizen defender, Pilot Knob, Mo.

Solomon Lax, citizen defender, Ironton, Mo.

Azariah Martin, Co. H, 47th Mo. Inf., Ironton, Mo.

Wm. F. Miller, Co. F, 47th Mo. Inf., Farmington, Mo.

James Moore, Co. I, 3rd M.S.M. Cav., Ellington, Mo.

David Murphy, Adjt. and Chief of Artillery, St. Louis, Mo.

Jno. Parkins, Co. L, 2nd M.S.M. Cav., Belgrade, Mo.

F.M. Parker, Co. A, 47th Mo. Inf., Cold Water, Mo.

J.C. Paullus, Sergt. Co. G, 47th Mo. Inf., Belleview, Mo.

B.B. Reagan, citizen defender, Ironton, Mo.

Geo. W. Rhodes, Corpl. Co. I, 3rd M.S.M. Cav., Shrum, Mo.

James W. Ross, Q.M. Dept., Fulton, Ill.

Tho. H. Russell, Corpl. Co. C, 3rd M.S.M. Cav., Belmont, Kas.

Claiborn C. Rust, Co. I, 47th Mo. Inf., Ironton, Mo.

Jno. Schwab, 2nd Lieut. Co. E, 47th Mo. Inf., Ironton, Mo.

Joshua Shaw, Co. I, 3rd M.S.M. Cav., Higdon, Mo.

Johnson M. Shell, Co. K, 3rd M.S.M. Cav., Lutesville, Mo.

Peter Shrum, Corpl. Co. I, 47th Mo. Inf., Sligo, Mo.

Merida P. Tate, 1st Lieut. Co. H, 47th Mo. Inf., Gainesville, Mo.

Damon J. Taylor, Co. G, 47th Mo. Inf., Piedmont, Mo.

Ferdinand O. Tennison, Co. D, 3rd M.S.M. Cav., Elvins, Mo.

Thos. J. Thompson, Co. I, 47th Mo. Inf., Higdon, Mo.

Henry Valle, citizen defender, Ironton, Mo.

Henry C. Wilkinson, 1st Sergt. Co. H, 47th Mo. Inf., Piedmont, Mo.

Edw. A. Wilkinson, Sergt. Co. H, 47th Mo. Inf., Fredericktown, Mo.

Jos. Wood, Co. I, 47th Mo. Inf., Mine La Motte, Mo.

Jno. W. Wynn, Co. A, 3rd M.S.M. Cav., Piedmont, Mo.

Fred Young, Co. K, 3rd M.S.M. Cav., Lutesville, Mo.

CONFEDERATE SURVIVORS

T.J. Buckner, Co. C, 8th Mo. Cav C.S.A., Thurman, Mo.

Jno. P. Dunklin, Jr., Co. C, 3rd Mo. Cav. C.S.A., Pocahontas, Ark.

Necrology

The following participants in the battle of Pilot Knob have passed away since our last meeting:

First Lieut. James Copp, Co. H, 3rd M.S.M. Cav., died at Norwood, Colo., March 14, 1905.

Sergt. Wm. F. Pritchett, Co. D, 3rd M.S.M. Cav., died at Vandalia, Mo., March 29, 1905

Private Frederick W. Page, Co. A, 3rd M.S.M. Cav., died at Ellsberry, Lincoln Co., Mo.

Private August Guenther, Co. K, 3rd M.S.M. Cav., died at Cape Girardeau, Mo., June 1, 1905.

Private Wm. Kohlmeyer, Co. F, 47th Mo. Inf., Died near Farmington, Mo., June 24, 1905.

Lieut. Jno. H. Delano, Co. E, 47th Mo. Inf., Died at Murphysboro, Ill., August 18, 1905.

Private John Copeland, Co. F, 47th Mo. Inf., Died at Ellington, Mo., August 24, 1905.

Private Francis Hailmann, Co. G, 1st M.S.M. Inf., died at the National Military Home, Kans., August 31st, 1905.

On the back page of the booklet was information regarding an Iron Mountain railroad route leading to the Pilot Knob Battlefield and to "Beautiful Arcadia Valley," which were reached by the "St. Louis, Iron Mountain & Southern Ry" via six trains daily in each direction.

FROM THE THIRD ANNUAL MEETING OF THE PILOT KNOB MEMORIAL ASSOCIATION ON THE FORTY-SECOND ANNIVERSARY OF THE BATTLE OF PILOT KNOB, SEPTEMBER 26TH, 27TH AND 28TH, 1906. ORIGINALLY PRINTED BY PRESS A.R. FLEMING PRINTING COMPANY, ST. LOUIS, MISSOURI.

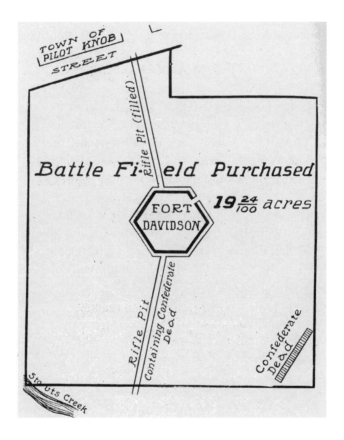

Part of battlefield purchased by Pilot Knob Memorial Association.

THE PILOT KNOB MEMORIAL ASSOCIATION

The third annual meeting of the Pilot Knob Memorial Association began in old Fort Davidson on Sept. 26th, 1906, with several hundred survivors and affiliated veterans present, and about one thousand visitors of a younger generation participating in the memorial exercises. The day was given over to informal fraternization and to viewing various points on the battlefield.

On Sept. 27th the Association was called to order by the President, Col. David Murphy, and the report of the Secretary, H.C. Wilkinson, and Corresponding Secretary, C.A. Peterson, acting historians of the Association, was rendered, giving the corrected casualty list on the Union side in the battle of Pilot Knob, Sept. 26th and 27th, 1864. A careful study of the Union losses has been made by the two Secretaries for the past six years, and the verified list, which is believed to be correct in every detail, was submitted as follows:

Killed in the Battle of Pilot Knob, Sept. 26th and 27th, 1864

Private Wm. Rector, Company 1 [I], 3rd M.S.M. Cavalry.
Corporal Francis T. Jeffries, Company E, 14th Iowa Infantry.
Private David W. McMillen, Company E, 14th Iowa Infantry.
Private Samuel W. Weir, Company C, 3rd M.S.M. Cavalry.
Corporal Benj. F. Turner, Company H, 3rd M.S.M. Cavalry.
Private Richard Estes, Company D, 3rd M.S.M. Cavalry.
Private John B. Tesreau, Company F, 50th Missouri Infantry.
Sergeant Isaiah B. West, Battery H, 2nd Missouri Light Artillery.
Private Elbert F. Hall, Battery H, 2nd Missouri Light Artillery.
Private Wm. F. Lee, Battery H, 2nd Missouri Light Artillery.
Citizen Charles W. Purcell.
Citizen Jacob Suda.
Citizen Beverly Russell (col.) [colored]
Citizen Robert Flynn (col.)

Killed, 14.

Mortally Wounded

Private Chas. Stamma, Company K, 3rd M.S.M. Cavalry; accidentally, right lung; wounded P.M. 26th, died Sept. 28th.
Private J. L. Williams, Company K, 3rd M.S.M. Cavalry; on Pilot Knob, lung; wounded P.M. 27th, died Sept. 28th.
Private J.W. Scroggins, Company C, 3rd M.S.M. Cavalry; on Pilot Knob, head; wounded P.M. 27th, died Sept. 28th.
Private Jonathan A. Epply, Company G, 47th Missouri Infantry; wounded P.M. 27th, died Sept. 29th.
Private Mathias Ditzen, Company G, 1st M.S.M. Infantry; in fort, body; wounded P.M. 27th, died Sept. 28th.

Private Conrad Herrenleben, Company G, 1st M.S.M. Infantry; in fort, body; wounded P.M. 27th, died Sept. 28th.

Private Bernhardt Weible, Company G, 1st M.S.M. Infantry; in fort, body; wounded P.M. 27th, died Oct. 10th.

Private James W. Lee, Battery H, 2nd Missouri Light Artillery; in fort, head; wounded P.M. 27th, died Sept. 30th.

Private Carrol Dennis, Company K, 3rd M.S.M. Cavalry; in fort, spine; wounded P.M. 27th, died Oct. 10th.

John Martin, citizen; in fort, head; wounded P.M. 27th, died Sept. 29th.

James Farrar, citizen (col.); in fort, loins; wounded P.M. 27th, died Sept. 28th.

Private John R. Cummings, Company C, 14th Iowa Infantry; right shoulder; wounded P.M. 27th, died Oct. 25th, at Cape Girardeau.

Private Henry A. Clem, Company D, 14th Iowa Infantry; near fort, right hip; wounded P.M. 27th, died Nov. 20th.

Private Lewis V. Tarelton, Company G, 47th Missouri Infantry; left leg; wounded P.M. 27th, died Nov. 1st.

Mortally wounded, 14.

Missing in Action—Probably Captured and Murdered

Private Chas. J. Thorpe, Company B, 14th Iowa Infantry.

Missing, not accounted for: 1.

Surviving Wounded—(In Hospitals.)

Private W.J. Bates, Company G, 47th Missouri Infantry; right leg.

Private Horatio Bean, Company E, 14th Iowa Infantry; right leg.

Private H.H. Brown, 47th Missouri Infantry; right hip.

Private Frederick Buch, Battery H, 2nd Missouri Light Artillery; head.

Private C.G. Burns, Company F, 47th Missouri Infantry; body.

Private Matthew Beckett, Company F, 47th Missouri Infantry; concussion.

Private Wm. Burris, Company D, 3rd M.S.M. Cavalry; right hip.

Sergeant Henry Bidewell, Company K, 3rd M.S.M. Cavalry; right knee.

Private Michael Bippus, Company G, 1st M.S.M. Infantry; right arm.

Private Jonathan Couch, Company K, 3rd M.S.M. Cavalry; right leg.

Private Richard Capps, Battery H, 2nd Missouri Light Artillery; burned.

Private James P. Doss, Company E, 47th Missouri Infantry; right cheek.

Private Casper Ernest, Company G, 1st M.S.M. Infantry; head.
Private F.M. Gaulden, Company F, 47th Missouri Infantry; right arm.
Private Harden Garner, Company G, 47th Missouri Infantry; foot.
Sergeant James A. Grieber, Company I, 3rd M.S.M. Cavalry; back.
Private John Hopper, Battery H, 2nd Missouri Light Artillery; contusion.
Private Elias Hopkins, Company H, 3rd M.S.M. Cavalry; fractured leg.
Private Henry Hilsman, Company G, 1st M.S.M. Infantry; neck.
Private Jonathan E. King, Battery H, 2nd Missouri Light Artillery; left hip.
Corporal Thos. M. King, Battery H, 2nd Missouri Light Artillery; left thigh.
Private John J. Lee, Company K, 3rd M.S.M. Cavalry; right arm.
Private Anthony Linville, Company L, 2nd M.S.M. Cavalry; contusion.
Private David Miller, Company G, 1st M.S.M. Infantry; eye.
Private John Merrit, Company F, 47th Missouri Infantry; forehead.
Sergeant Josiah J. Montgomery, Battery H, 2nd Missouri Light Artillery; burned.
Sergeant Wm. Nevin, Company K, 3rd M.S.M. Cavalry; right hip.
Private Cornelius O'Shae, Company K, 3rd M.S.M. Cavalry; contusion.
Private Anthony O'Hara, Company F, 47th Missouri Infantry; right side.
Private Henry Ruwe, Company H, 3rd M.S.M. Infantry; shoulder.
Private Erhardt Roedel, Company G, 1st M.S.M. Infantry; right arm.
Private Edwin Steele, Company A, 3rd M.S.M. Cavalry; neck.
Private A.B. Stamps, Battery H, 2nd Missouri Light Artillery; burned.
First Lieutenant Smith Thompson, Company D, 14th Iowa Infantry; left thigh.
First Lieutenant Geo. Tetley, Company E, 47th Missouri Infantry; left shoulder.
Private David J. Taylor, Company H, 14th Iowa Infantry; left arm.
Private John Wade, Company C, 14th Iowa Infantry; ankle.
Private Geo. W. Williams, Company G, 47th Missouri Infantry; right ankle.
Private Thos. Willis, Company H, 3rd M.S.M. Cavalry; right leg.
Citizen Frederick Dettmer; shoulder.
Citizen Armistead Holman; right elbow.
Citizen Geo. W. Horn; neck and face.
Citizen G. Menden; ankle.
Citizen Frank Steneke; both knees.

Wounded, 44.

Total casualties, 73.

Slightly Wounded.—(Not in Hospitals.)

Major James Wilson, 3rd M.S.M. Cavalry.
Captain Herman A. Miles, Company C, 14th Iowa Infantry.
Captain P.L. Powers, Company H, 47th Missouri Infantry.
Lieutenant Joshua Mason, enrolled militia.
Private Samuel Rhodes, Company K, 3rd M.S.M. Cavalry.
Private H.Q. Collins, Company K, 3rd M.S.M. Cavalry.
Sergeant Spencer Stevens, Company D, 3rd M.S.M. Cavalry.
Private Isaac H. Dillon, Company D, 3rd M.S.M. Cavalry.
Private Wm. C.H. Burbridge, Company C, 3rd M.S.M. Cavalry.

Note.—The foregoing list agrees, practically, in numbers with official reports following the battle, but careful analysis has changed the personnel of the list greatly. Of the wounded, H.H. Brown cannot be identified, though his name stands on hospital record; Hardin Garner went to Rolla before going into hospital, and Joshua Mason would have remained in hospital for treatment, but feared murder, so sought concealment and treatment at his home.

Purchase of the Battlefield

The Corresponding Secretary reported the progress of the movement inaugurated one year ago to purchase the heart of the battlefield, containing old Fort Davidson and the graves of most of those, especially Confederates, who fell in the battle. A tract of nearly 20 acres was bought on Dec. 15th, 1905, and stands deeded to Thomas Ewing, Jr., August Gehner and Cyrus A. Peterson, associate members of the Association, for which $1,444.00 was paid. Of this amount $794.00 has been paid in, on subscriptions, and $650.00 rests as a voluntary loan on the part of two members of the Association. This is the only battlefield west of the Mississippi River now preserved from desecration and the following are the persons who have generously assisted in this patriotic act:

Subscriptions Paid in for Purchase of Battlefield

$100.00 each—
Thos. Ewing, Jr., and C.A. Peterson $200.00

$50.00 each—

August Gehner, D.M. Houser, David Murphy   150.00

$25.00 each—

B.B. Cahoon, Sr., Isaac H. Dillon, Daniel B. Dyer,
   Henry King, Wm. L. Morsey, Samuel B. Rowe,
   C.P. Walbridge   175.00

$15.00—

H.B. Milks   15.00

$10.00 each—

D.I. Bushnell, W.J. Campbell, Azariah Martin,
   Julius Pitzman, Wm. T. Shaw, Edwin H. Tyler   60.00

$5.00 each

J.R. Adams, Julius A. Betzel, John Boyle, Geo. G.
   Bryan Post G.A.R. No. 254 [should be 284,
   Belegrade Post], A.R. Chandler, John A.
   Donaldson, David P. Floyd, Wm. T. Gay, Ed.
   Helber, Jacob Helber, Randolph James, John S.
   Luthy, H.Y. Mabrey, John Newman, Thos.
   Newman, W.F. Parks, Picket Post G.A.R. No. 215,
   W.L.H. Silliman, Frank Schutle, Lewis W. Sutton,
   John L. Thomas, Thos. J. Thompson, Washington
   Underwood, H.C. Wilkinson, Mrs. M.E. Wray,
   H.J. Wray   130.00

$3.00—

Thos. Cook   3.00

$2.50 each—

B.F. Barrett, H.C. Draper, Artemus Shattuck, W.C.
   Shattuck   10.00

$2.00

Henry Anderson, S.U. Branstetter, E.P. Gardner, Jacob
   Haller, G.W. Rhodes   10.00

$1.50

John J. Chadwick   1.50

$1.00 each—

F.M. Adams, Warren Alexander, R.L. Atchison, James F.
   Bennett, W.H. Cameron, T.F. Chamberlain, C.C.
   Chandler, Thos. Creech, Thos. T. Dalton, D.D. Durr,
   D.H. Easter, W.Z. Evans, Thos. Fortune, F.W. Hale, B.
   P. Hale, Loyd G. Harris, Thos. H. Henderson, Wm. P.

Hiller, E.K. Hopkins, W.C. Ion, Abram M. Lafferty,
Thos. Lang, W.R. Lang, Henry Lenger, Miss D.J.B.
Mayo, Martin and Mueller, J.D. Merritt, Michael
Mueller, Geo. L. Murray, John E. Privett, F.A.
Robinson, F.C. Schultz, Peter Shrum, W.N. Vannoy,
Benj. Woodruff, Mrs. Sarah Woodruff, Roy York.   37.00
50 cents each—
W.H. Farrow, E.A. Kelsey, J.F. Keough, J.B. Kerr,
C.A. Schucknecht   37.00
[printing repeats "37.00"; should be "2.25"]

Paid in $794.00
Still due   650.00

Total $1,444.00

ELECTION OF OFFICERS

Nominations were made and the following officers were elected for the ensuing year, viz.:

David Murphy, President, St. Louis, Mo.

H.C. Wilkinson, Secretary, Piedmont, Mo.

C.A. Peterson, Corresponding Secretary, St. Louis, Mo.

*Henry S. Carroll, Treasurer, St. Louis, Mo.

Vice-Presidents—Wm. J. Campbell, Oakville, Iowa; H.B. Milks, Leon, Kan.; Sam B. Rowe, Rolla, Mo.; T.M. Montgomery, Akard, Mo.; Wm. H. Smith, Park Place, Ore.; James H. Nations, Womack, Mo.; Wm. T. Gay, Ironton, Mo.

Assistant Secretaries—Hugo Hoffbauer, Buffalo, Iowa; John A. Rice, Braswell, Mo.; James C. Steakley, Patton, Mo.; Charles Biehle, St. Louis, Mo.; James M. Travis, Greenfield, Mo.; Thos. Ewing, Jr. 67 Wall street, New York, N.Y.; John S. Luthy, Pilot Knob, Mo.

[*]Died Nov. 20th, 1906.

Thomas Clement Fletcher, colonel of the 31st Missouri Infantry and the 47th Missouri Infantry and Brevet Brigadier General—second field officer in rank at the Battle of Pilot Knob, Sept. 27, 1864. Born January 22, 1827. Died March 25, 1899.

At 2 P.M. Hon. John L. Thomas, a life-long friend of Col. Thomas C. Fletcher, was introduced to the audience and delivered the following oration on the life and public services of Col. Fletcher:

ORATION OF HON. JOHN L. THOMAS

When a few days ago I consented to speak to you to-day of Governor Fletcher and his public services, I hesitated for a while as to how I should proceed. I knew my audience would be composed mostly of old Union soldiers, and while some of them would know what I had been, there would probably be some present who would not know. I finally concluded to take you into my confidence and tell you where I once stood in the past.

Prior to and during the Civil War I was a State's Rights Democrat. I then sincerely believed that while there was no positive constitutional provision authorizing secession, the central government had no lawful power to compel by force a state to remain in the Union against the consent of a majority of its citizens. I was born in Missouri of parents who moved from Virginia in 1826, and my environment and all my associations were intensely Southern.

Governor Fletcher was also born in Missouri, his parents being from Maryland and his environment and associations, too, were intensely Southern. He became, however, a disciple of Thomas H. Benton, and hence was soon dominated by anti-slavery ideas and by an intense love of the Union. He and I thus were antipodes in politics. But looking backward from my viewpoint now, I tell you on this occasion, that I most heartily rejoice and thank my god that my conceptions of the power of the States and the National Government did not prevail, but that, on the contrary, the sovereignty of the Union has been established beyond recall. I see now clearly what it seems to me at this time we all ought to have seen forty-five years ago, that this country could not be divided at all, but especially not by a line running east and west; that one division would be the precursor of another, until we would have as many petty republics as we have States and that these States would be continually involved in strife and often in armed conflicts. This much of myself; and I have told you this in order for you to understand and appreciate what I shall say.

The first time I ever saw Thomas Clement Fletcher was Sept. 25th, 1849, at a public meeting at Hillsboro, when Miss. M. Clara Honey, who afterwards became his wife, presented him, on behalf of the Sons of Temperance, a beautiful banner, with an appropriate address, which he accepted graciously from the fair hands of his fiancé. I was a boy then, but Mr. Fletcher was a man, he being six years older than myself. Our first acquaintance was in 1854, and after that we became intimate friends, riding the large Judicial Circuits of the State together in the practice of law. From the first we seemed to be congenial spirits, and while we differed in politics we were always warm friends, before, during and after the war, and what I shall have to say of him here to-day will be from the standpoint of a friend.

His Place in History

It is too soon, probably, to forecast the place Governor Fletcher will occupy in the history of this State. It is said contemporaries cannot write just biographies. They may be, and too often are, biased either by prejudice or friendship, and we cannot tell positively the niches posterity will make for the worthy sons of our proud State. There is no reason, however, why a friend should not, on an occasion like this, where his comrades in suffering and in glory have met to celebrate his and their achievements on this historic battlefield, predict how high Governor Fletcher's niche will be in the temple of fame. At least there is no reason why he should not state how high he thinks and believes that niche ought to be.

His Part in the Battle of Pilot Knob

I shall not speak of his military career. That task has been done by others more capable than I. I will simply add that when the battle of Pilot Knob occurred, forty-two years ago, Colonel Fletcher was the Republican candidate for Governor, and General Price, knowing he was in Fort Davidson, was extremely anxious to capture him and, thus, as he thought, prevent his election. General Price had with him Thomas C. Reynolds, who had been, in 1860, elected Lieutenant-Governor of this State, and Governor Jackson having died in 1862, Reynolds claimed to be the Governor, and it was a part of Price's programme to take Jefferson City, install Reynolds as Governor and order an election for his successor in November, 1864. The contest in this valley, September 27, 1864, emphasized, in a striking way, the fierce struggle for the mastery between the Union and secession forces. Col. Fletcher was the colonel of a regiment in this fort, fighting for the Union and at the same time he was the candidate of the Union party for Governor of the State. Over there in Arcadia was Thomas C. Reynolds, claiming to be the Governor by virtue of his election in 1860, and at the same time he was fighting to make Missouri a member of the Confederate States. The question whether Reynolds should be governor of our state as a member of the Southern Confederacy or Fletcher as a member of the Federal Union was squarely submitted to arbitrament of the sword on that historic day at this historic place. The Union force won; Price was foiled; and though he marched his army through the State, destroying property worth $10,000,000 as he himself says, and costing many lives on both sides, he was, in the last days of October, driven from the State and Fletcher became the first elected Republican Governor of a slave State and the first native born Governor of Missouri. He was inaugurated January 2, 1865.

Personal Characteristics

My friend Fletcher was a superb specimen of manhood. He was my ideal of manly beauty. He was tall, erect and robust, and with his suave manners and commanding address was easily noted among the most distinguished. From early manhood he was a progressive man. Always and everywhere he was found on the firing line of advancing civilization. He was no laggard along any line. Were agriculture and horticulture to be improved; were mines to be developed; were factories to be introduced; was the system of education to be improved, this native son of Missouri was always found standing in the front ranks and calling to the people to advance to something better and higher in the future than anything they had had in the past, and his voice and work were potent for the advance that actually came.

He was a man true to his convictions of right. Reared in a community intensely pro-slavery and by parents who owned slaves, he became before the war an anti-slavery advocate. He joined the Republican party, born of the Kansas controversy, in its avowed purpose to exclude slavery from the territory of the United States. Free speech, free soil and free men became his battle cry and no one born since the war can appreciate the courage it required in 1860 in Missouri to openly advocate the non-extension of slavery to the territories. But this Governor Fletcher did. He belonged to a "Wide Awake" Republican Club, the first one, it is said, organized in a slave State, and the name of the club is an index of its character. He was at all times a wide awake man.

He was a delegate to the Chicago convention in 1860 that nominated Mr. Lincoln. Outside of the large cities the Republican party had but few adherents in this state at that time. Governor Fletcher rejected the opinions of his father and his friends to follow his own convictions of right as he saw the right. He chose to bear the odium of a "black Republican," for all Republicans in 1860 were universally called "black Republicans" by the southern people in Missouri, and everywhere else, to follow his conscience.

In taking this course he also knew that political preferment in this state was out of the question, and so far as the wisest could then discern, the time of ostracism of an anti-slavery man would extend far beyond that generation and the succeeding one. It is true five years changed the whole aspect of affairs but no man foresaw in 1860 the revolution that came so soon. It was therefore not only to his social, but his political interest not to break with the pro-slavery party.

It was said of Mr. Fletcher that he sometimes vacillated, but when we look into his record we find him weak, if weak at all, on questions he regarded as unimportant. The fact that he became a Republican and took the stump for Mr. Lincoln in 1860 in this State, proves him to have been a strong man when his conscience approved a principle he regarded as eternally right. He believed slavery wrong, and he laid upon that altar, for a time, all his social and political hopes of preferment. I affirm he was a strong man on essentials though he might sometimes seem to waver on non-essentials. And even this weakness, if it was a weakness, was due to another as noble trait as distinguishes man from the brute, and that was his kindness and human sympathy. Who can say he ever erred in giving his kindness the victory over his firmness in matters he regarded not of over mastering importance.

Governor Fletcher was an altruist of the best type. He spent much of his life in the service of others. Money getting and money saving was not his forte. What money he had was at the disposal of his friends if they asked it. He would quit his business and spend hours at a time to render favors to those he knew. I can safely affirm from what I knew of him personally, that but few men, if any, in the State, have done more "thank-y' jobs" for others than this unselfish man. He spent so much time in the service of others, he neglected his own affairs, the result of which was he lived and died a poor man. And yet he did not escape the slanderer's tongue nor libeler's pen in the days of his greatest service to the State, when party rancor ran higher than it ever did before or has since. But he bore it all without complaint. He had faith that time would vindicate his name and protect his honor, and it has vindicated him.

Governor Fletcher was a liberal man. He opposed the adoption of the Constitution of 1865, and in a year after his inauguration as governor he began his recommendations for the modification of the restrictive provisions of that instrument. This he continued to do to the end of his term, when, in his last message, he urged that all these provisions be abolished, and when constitutional amendments to accomplish this result were submitted to the people in 1870 he gave them his hearty and active support, and nearly all of his own party went with him, and these measures were triumphantly carried by more than one hundred and ten thousand majority. Thus in six years after the war closed, largely through his conservative course, the State had been reconstructed and those who wore the gray put upon the same political plane with those who wore the blue; and henceforth they were to march forward shoulder to shoulder in the development of our imperial state.

In 1867 he wrote a letter to E.A. Hickman that he would be glad to co-operate with him in the establishment of a home for the widows and orphans of Confederate soldiers at Independence. In that letter he used this noble language.

"The widows and orphans have never appealed to me in vain when it was in my power to aid them.

My sympathy for suffering humanity does not admit of inquiry on my part as to whose widows and orphans are to be succored; it is sufficient for me to know they are widows and fatherless to entitle them to my sympathy and aid."

No man can use such words as these whose heart is not in the right place. His sympathy was as broad as humanity itself, and while he fought four years for the Union, and felt that to secure the fruits of the war it was necessary, for a time, to deprive those who had taken up arms on the other side, of the right of suffrage, at no time did he bear malice against those Southern men who gallantly fought for what they believed to be right. In his inaugural he says: "Behind us we leave the wrecks of old institutions and all the bitter memories of the terrible past, retaining only the lessons of wisdom our experience of them has taught us. Before us, glowing with promise and fruitful with hope, is the mighty future."

Again he says: "Let us welcome to a participation in our coming prosperity and greatness as a State all who unite with us in upholding and defending the Constitution of the United States and of the State of Missouri."

Governor Fletcher was an optimist. This I knew from my earliest acquaintance with him. This trait glowed preeminently in his inaugural address, January 2, 1865. When he became Governor there was much to appall the soul of the most heroic. We had had four years of a most devastating war; that war was an internecine one in the strictest sense. Brother was arrayed against brother; father against son; neighbor against neighbor. The contending hostile forces had traversed nearly every foot of Missouri territory and her soil had been drenched in the fraternal blood of her sons. The railroads had been badly crippled and two or more tiers of our border counties from the Missouri river to New Madrid were almost one vast desolation; taxes had not been paid in many sections for years; the State's credit was almost gone and the intensest [*sic*] passion of anger and hatred rankled in the hearts of both combatants. The State government was to be reorganized; the angry passions engendered by the war were to be calmed and the participants in that dreadful conflict were to be invited to return to their homes and together asked to rebuild the waste places; the credit of the State was to be put on a secure foundation; the industrial system of the State, due to the emancipation of the slaves, was to be readjusted to the new order of things; the educational system was to be made to conform to the new conditions and the State was to be again put on the highway of peace and progress. History furnishes but few instances of so many delicate and difficult questions as confronted Governor Fletcher's administration at its inauguration. But in the midst of all these disheartening conditions, Governor Fletcher's inaugural breathes the spirit of optimism through and through. He could see nothing but a bright future for his native State he loved so well, and his words and influence helped materially to shape that future and make it bright. If the questions confronting him were many and difficult, his opportunity was great, an opportunity that comes to few men in this world. He was at the head of the State government at the end of a revolution that ushered in a new era. The old regime was to be replaced by a new order of things. Up to 1865, Missouri had been a slave State, henceforth freedom for all, black and white alike, was to be the watchword. How my friend aided in laying the new foundations of this disenthralled State it becomes my pleasant task to relate. Prior to 1865 and for ages past, parties to suits could not testify in their own favor upon the hypothesis that an interested party could not be relied on to tell the truth, thus stigmatizing the whole human race. This rule, hoary with age, was changed in 1865, and parties to suits were made competent witnesses in their own favor. This provision has remained and is the law today.

The Credit of the State

The debt of the State, principal and interest, January 1, 1865, amounted to more than $36,000,000. The State virtually had no financial standing in the markets of the world. In his inaugural address Governor Fletcher took strong ground for the restoration and preservation of the State's credit. He urged the Legislature to adopt such measures "as become a people whose honesty was unshaken by misfortune, who are resolved to pay their debts." That body, February 15, 1865, by joint resolution, citing this patriotic language, declared it to be "the fixed and unalterable purpose" of the people it represented to preserve the faith of the State and to satisfy the demands of its creditors "to the fullest requirement," and a committee was appointed to report a plan to accomplish that result. That committee reported a plan to the adjourned session 1865–66. Governor Fletcher sent in a special message February 28, 1866, in which he says: "No Missourian possessing due pride in the rising greatness of our State would permit the blighting effects of repudiation to tarnish our fair name and darken our future, and many, I fear, fail to see that the effect of refusing to pay a part, however small, of our debts, when we have the ability to do so, is virtually repudiation." He then continues in this spirited language: "I beseech you to take such steps at this time as will relieve our State from liability to such a charge even by implication." And in six days thereafter the General Assembly responded to this appeal by passing an act to fund the State's debt and to provide for the payment of the principal and interest. The credit of the State continued to be an object of the Governor's solicitude afterwards, and by the time he retired from office in January, 1869, he could truthfully say he had aided "in the transformation of the public finances and credit from an almost hopeless embarrassment to an unquestioned standing by the reduction of the debt to a sum which may be carried with its weight scarcely perceptible." He had aided in reducing the debt from $36,000,000 to $18,000,000 and in providing means to pay interest. On this important question Governor Fletcher's record is flawless and will remain a prominent monument to his fame.

Education

Prior to the war the underlying theory of the public school system of the State was that free schools were intended mainly for the education of children of indigent parents. This theory was based on the Constitution of 1820, which provided that one school or more in each township, as soon as practicable and necessary, should be established, "were the poor shall be taught gratis." The statutes enacted to carry out that constitutional provision authorized school officers to engage teachers and pay them out of the income of funds derived from the sale of the lands donated by Congress for schools; from escheated estates and fines imposed for crimes with twenty-five per cent of the State revenue, as far as that income went, and to raise the deficit by rate bills issued against those who patronized the schools, and these officers were clothed with authority to exempt poor persons from these rate bills.

The result of this system was that, as a rule, teachers were not employed for a longer term than the public money, derived as above, would sustain. No taxation, except in the City of St. Louis, on the property of teachers or for the current expenses of schools was authorized not even by a vote of the people. The law forbade anyone, under a penalty of a maximum fine of $500.00 or a maximum imprisonment of six months, or both, to keep or teach a school for the instruction of negroes, free or slave.

The State University, prior to the war and even prior to 1867, had to rely on its maintenance wholly on the income derived from the sale of lands donated by the general government for that institution and on private subscriptions. The State had not contributed anything. The curriculum of the University did not include agriculture or mechanic arts, law, medicine or the military art. This was the public school system when the war broke out in 1861. In 1864 the Legislature provided that school trustees might raise by taxation $150.00 in each district to defray the expenses of schools, but this was not made compulsory and was never put in operation.

This was the school system as it existed when Thomas C. Fletcher became Governor in January, 1865. In his inaugural address he advised that the superstructure of that system should be different from that which previously prevailed. Accordingly the General Assembly went to work to make the educational system conform to the new order of things, and an act for this purpose was passed and approved March 29th, 1865. This act made an advance that amounted to a revolution. It made the raising of sufficient means by taxation to maintain schools in the districts at least four months in the year compulsory, and it authorized the continuance of the schools for a longer period by a vote of the people. The importance of this provision is emphasized by its having been made permanent by the Constitution of 1875. It is still the law and is here to stay.

This act also provided for free schools for colored children. Here was a complete reversal of the old system. This provision presented a sharp contrast between what had been unlawful in the past and what was made not only lawful, but commendable, in the future. When Governor Fletcher retired from office in 1869 he knew that 33,619 colored children substantially all in the State of school age, were either in public or private schools. What a glorious consummation that was.

Then came the Constitution of 1865 which uprooted the old theory of public schools by declaring that "the General Assembly shall establish and maintain public schools for the gratuitous instruction of *all persons* in the State between the ages of five and twenty-one years"; and this went into the Constitution of 1875 with the modification that the school age was fixed between six and twenty years, instead of five and twenty-one. Under the inspiration of the new school law, this constitutional provision and of the new era over three thousand new school houses were built in 1867 and 1868, and these houses were generally of a much better class than the school houses of the past.

Governor Fletcher made the State University a special object of solicitude on his part, urging the establishment of departments of agriculture and mechanic arts and law, a normal department and a department for military instruction. The General Assembly by Act, March 11, 1867, made an annual appropriation of one and three-quarters percent of the revenue of the State, after deducting the one-fourth set aside for public schools, for the support of the University, and $10,000 was appropriated to repair the buildings. This was the first appropriation of money for this purpose made by the State in its whole history. The normal and military departments were established and put in operation before the end of Governor Fletcher's term of office, and he lived to see all his fond hopes, as to the other departments, fulfilled. The University is today what he urged forty years ago it should be.

Slave Made Free

But the act of Governor Fletcher which gave him the greatest pleasure was the proclamation of the freedom of 115,000 slaves in the State, January 11, 1865. The Constitutional Convention, then sitting at St. Louis, on that day, passed the ordinance of emancipation and by a separate resolution requested the Governor to issue a proclamation of freedom. This he did the same day. The language and spirit of this State paper is an index to the deep feeling of the Governor on the subject of slavery and the inexpressible joy he experienced in declaring the slaves of the State free. He proclaimed "that henceforth and forever no person within the jurisdiction of this State shall be subject 'to any abridgment of liberty, except such as the law may prescribe for the common good, or know no master but God.'"

In the next few days he received telegrams of congratulations from the Governors of Iowa, Wisconsin, Michigan, Kansas, Nebraska, Pennsylvania, Massachusetts, Vermont, Maine, Ohio, Tennessee, from the Legislature of Illinois, from the Speaker of the House of Representatives at Washington and from the Secretary of War.

These telegrams must have been very gratifying and inspiring to the Governor and the people. To give you an idea of their spirit and tone, I quote a few. Governor Stone of Iowa said: "Hail! Hail! Free Missouri! Thrice tried by fire and sword, the metal is as the pure gold."

Governor Crawford of Kansas exclaimed: "Free Missouri! Thank God."

Governor Curtin of Pennsylvania greeted Missouri and welcomed her as a disenthralled sister "redeemed in the agony of the Nation."

Governor Corey of Maine welcomed the State "to the blessings of free institutions after forty years of wandering in the wilderness."

Governor Fenton of New York said: "God bless freed Missouri."

Speaker Colfax of the National House of Representatives rejoiced that Missouri had "broken every yoke and let the oppressed go free."

As for myself, Southern born and Southern bred as I was, if I had been asked what act of glory I would perform I would have chosen the issuance of the proclamation of the freedom that opened the door of hope to 115,000 slaves, bidding them to go forth as free men and women and assuring them that henceforth they need call no one master but God, and to receive those telegrams of sympathy and thanksgiving. This proclamation and his inaugural address made Governor Fletcher a national figure.

The Slave Code Abolished

In Governor Fletcher's inaugural he reminded the General Assembly that the amendments to the Constitution would require "the erasure of the word 'slave' from our statutes, the abolition of the distinction of color in the law relating to crimes and punishments and the abrogation of all laws for the fostering and protection of the interests of slavery." Thereupon the Legislature by act, February 20, 1865, after reciting the ordinance of emancipation and the Governor's proclamation of freedom, repealed Chapter 150, R.S. 1855, entitled "Slaves," containing three articles and seventy-eight sections in all; chapter 114 entitled "Free Negroes and Mulatoes," containing forty-one sections, and chapter 121 entitled "Patrols."

Besides these whole chapters swept from the statute books, this act repealed or modified ninety-four sections of various other chapters in order to eliminate the last vestige of the slave code from the statutes. One cannot read this act without realizing how thoroughly our whole system of laws had been saturated with slavery and its attendant adjuncts. The promiscuous sections repealed or modified by this act related to crimes and punishments, dower, habeas corpus, witnesses, executors and administrators and other subjects.

Prior to 1865 a negro or mulatto could not could not be a witness for or against a white person. Negroes were, prior to that date, punished for the most part for crimes committed by them by whipping, the number of lashes being usually thirty-nine. The whipping post for whites had not existed in this State for twenty years, but for the negro it did not finally disappear till February 20, 1865.

The General Assembly passed another act, which was approved by Governor Fletcher, February 20, 1865, which provided for the marriage of negroes and legitimatizing of their children born in slavery. While marriage among slaves was common, the marital relation, in fact, scarcely existed with them. It is one of the concomitants of slavery to make the family relations of husband and wife and parent and child of slight importance. By this act the sanctity of the family and home was assured to this unfortunate race; and no more in this State were husbands and wives, parents and children, to be torn asunder by those who estimate the most sacred relations of life on the basis of the dollar.

Besides these specific measures adopted during the most critical period in the history of the State, Governor Fletcher found time to call the attention of the law-making power to other important matters. He asked for a Board of Immigration and it was granted as early as 1865. He recommended the creation of the office of Commissioner of Insurance, and that was done soon after he retired from office, He urged the establishment of district normal schools and a school of mines, and these came in 1870—less than two years from the end of his term. His urged compulsory education, and that is the law today. He, in his strenuous efforts to extend the Southwest branch (now Frisco) and Iron Mountain roads, with a prophetic eye looked to the South and Southwest for the source of the commerce of St. Louis and Missouri.

The railroads were disposed of during his administration to parties, who were required to change their gauge to conform to the gauge of the connecting lines and to complete the roads then only partially built. By this means the mileage of the railroads of the State was increased in four years from 826 miles to 1394 of finished roads, besides 569 more in the process of construction in 1869, when the Governor presented his last message. All this was accomplished without a dollar of additional cost to the State.

The Eads and Quincy bridges over the Fathers of Waters, and the St. Charles and Kansas City bridges over the Missouri river were enterprises recommended by him and adopted while he was in office. And last, though not least, he never forgot his comrades in arms, their widows and orphans. He prayed that they be made the special objects of the State's care and gratitude.

This gives you the conditions Governor Fletcher had to meet and how he met them. He did not bring about these grand results alone by any means. No one pretends he did that. All I mean to affirm is that he stood in the front ranks, nay as the leader of those who did bring them about.

A revolution brought Thomas Clement Fletcher to the gubernatorial chair at a time when the institutions of sixty years, nurtured under the baneful influence of slave labor and a slave code, had fallen to pieces, and had to be reconstructed on the basis of freedom; at a time when the credit of the State was gone; the State devastated, and the resources of the people badly crippled; at a time when the passions of men had arrayed them into two hostile, radical camps to assail him from all sides; at a time when a conservative man and a steady hand was required. A new adjustment was demanded. The State was to step from the old to the new. Governor Fletcher, liberal and conservative, was there with steady purpose, to lead in this work of reconstruction and readjustment. How well he performed his part, I think may safely be left to posterity.

He entered office January 2, 1865, when all was chaos and confusion, the war still in progress, martial law in force and the passions of men at white heat by four years of the bloodiest civil war the world ever saw, and he left it January 8, 1869, the anniversary of the Battle of New Orleans, with the full assurance that law and order had been restored and the State, rehabilitated and disenthralled, had been securely put upon the highway of that marvelous progress which has come to her beyond the dreams of the most sanguine. And lifting the veil of the future, he, in his parting words, exclaimed: "Upon the virtue and intelligence of the people I rest my hopes of the attainment of a still higher and better destiny; and above all my hopes for our future as a people is radiant in the faith, which has been strengthened and enlarged amid the storms of State, that liberty and justice will be upheld by the protecting care of God."

I am glad I have had an opportunity to say a good word for my friend. It is a debt I owe him, for in the dark days of that awful war, when I was in trouble he heard my appeal and nobly and generously came to my relief, and this arm shall fall from its shoulder blade and this tongue shall cleave to the roof of my mouth ere I forget him or fail to defend his good name. He was a patriot and a pure man. Love of country and love of man dominated his whole nature. He was prouder that he was an American than that he was a Missourian; not that he loved Missouri less, but his country more. In his public and private relations he was scrupulously honest, and if to be right on all public questions is a gauge of statesmanship, he was a statesman. Read his messages and learn how many of his recommendations have become the foundation stones of our institutions. And when at last he came to lay down his burdens and go to "that bourne from whence no traveler returns," he could calmly look back to a life whose sole inspiration was to help his fellows and on days well spent. *Requiescat in Pace.*

(Note—A debt of thanks is due Judge Thomas from the Pilot Knob Memorial Association for his able exposition of the character of Governor Fletcher, probably the ablest and most self-sacrificing statesman who ever presided over the affairs of Missouri, but whose reputation was murderously slandered for more than thirty years by a gang who held political power in the State and contrived to wreck much of the good work mapped out and begun by Governor Fletcher.—Editor).

Address of Hon. Marion E. Rhodes

Hon. Marion E. Rhodes, Member of Congress from the Thirteenth Missouri District, and author of the bill to make this battlefield a National Military Park, was next introduced, and delivered the following address:

Mr. Chairman, Ladies and Gentlemen:—It is both a pleasure and an honor for me to be permitted to appear before this splendid audience, on the forty-second anniversary of the battle of Pilot Knob.

Forty-two years ago today, in this beautiful Arcadia valley, and between these mountains of granite, history was being made in Missouri. I wish to say, however, this important event, in the history of our beloved State and in the history of the civil war, took place before I was born. When a child, at my grandmother's knee, down here in Southeast Missouri, in old Bollinger County, where my ancestors have lived for more than half a century; I first heard the story of the battle of Pilot Knob. I had in this battle two uncles. I grew up in a neighborhood in which several old soldiers lived, who participated in this battle. I have heard the old citizens of our neighborhood tell of the awful roar of those cannon that were planted within these walls of earth, and on yonder hillside, which struck terror to the hearts of women and children, and caused the blood of brave men to run cold. Hence, I have known something of the battle of Pilot Knob all the days of my life.

I deem it both fitting and proper, that as we have met today under the auspices of the Pilot Knob Memorial Association, to celebrate the forty-second anniversary of this most important battle, that we take a retrospective view of that part of the history of the civil war which was fought in the State of Missouri. To begin with, Missouri was the very borderland between the North and the South. A reliable historian states that the greater number of battles were fought in Missouri than in any other State in the Union. Not the greatest battles, mark you, but a greater number of battles; among which was the battle of Pilot Knob. Here let us not fail to do honor to Gen. Lyon and his brave men who won lasting fame for themselves, and a decisive advantage for the cause of freedom and the perpetuation of the Union, by saying that the battle of Wilson's Creek, was perhaps the most important battle fought in Missouri during the civil war.

The past two years, I have been especially interested in a certain matter of legislation now pending before the United States Congress affecting a particular class of our Missouri soldiers of the civil war, and in my research I have found it necessary to examine a great many of the civil war records which are in the Congressional Library at Washington. In my study of these records, I have been astonished to see how the immortal Lincoln studied the Missouri situation during that awful conflict. Lincoln kept Missouri under his watchful eye at all times during the war. He made a special agreement with Governor Gamble of Missouri, in 1861, which resulted in 40,000 militiamen being called into the service. I here wish to say, the moral effect of this whole matter had much to do toward preventing Missouri from going out of the Union in 1861. Subsequent agreements and the calling of a large number of militia into active service, triumphantly saved Missouri to the Union. In truth and in fact, President Lincoln from the White House in Washington, conceived the idea which resulted in holding Missouri in the Union. He knew that Missouri with respect to her geographical situation, her rivers, her lines of railroad and important cities, was the very key to the whole war area west of the Mississippi, hence, the importance of holding it.

But I must now get back to the history of the battle of Pilot Knob. Historians agree, I believe, this battle was fought September 26th, 27th and 28th, 1864, between the Union forces, consisting of about 700 veterans and 300 minute men commanded by Brig. Gen. Thomas Ewing, and ably assisted by the distinguished chairman of this meeting, Col. David Murphy, and others; and a Confederate force of about 15,000 men commanded by Gen. Sterling Price.

It is well that we here remember the circumstances heading up to this memorable battle, fought by two such unequal opposing forces. Gen. Price had been driven from Missouri during the earlier part of the war, and the authority of the Federal Government maintained. Matters had so shaped themselves that Gen. Price decided during the summer of 1864 to make a final effort to regain Missouri. He accordingly planned his second invasion of the State with St. Louis and Jefferson City as the objective points. He believed he could capture these strongholds, because large numbers of the regulars had been drawn from the State in 1863 and 1864, and sent to relieve the situation in the South; and the matter of local defense was left largely to the militia of Missouri. St. Louis and Jefferson cities were important, because of their geographical advantage and the munitions of war they contained.

Gen. Price left Camden, Arkansas, near the latter part of August, 1864, with more than 15,000 men, the very flower of his great army, intending to invade Missouri. His army consisted of three divisions, commanded by three able generals, viz.: Gen. Fagan, Gen. Marmaduke and Geo. [sic] Joe Shelby. Strange as it may seem, Gen. Rosecranz [sic] who was at the head of the Union forces in Missouri, failed to discover that Gen. Price had penetrated Missouri until he was near Fredericktown. The fact is, Gen. Price skillfully deluded the Union forces into the belief that he would enter the State in Southwest Missouri, with Springfield as his objective point, thus diverting their attention from Southeast Missouri.

This, ladies and gentlemen, is the reason why Gen. Ewing with 1,000 men, was hastily forced to meet a great army of 15,000 men.

I imagine now, I can see that army making its way up this beautiful valley, with no other thought than an easy victory. To their surprise each assault was met with heavy repulse. All day long, forty-two years ago today, the fighting continued. Gen. Ewing commanding his little band of a thousand gallant heroes within the walls of this splendid old fort, keeping up the fight until night fall; then by one of the most strategetic [*sic*] movements recorded in military history, withdrew in safety and made his way to Rolla and thence into the interior of the State. Lack of time prevents me from describing more minutely the battle and the retreat, which began on the night of the 27th and which lasted for about three days.

Other speakers present, who have a vivid recollection of those turbulent days, and who were eye witnesses on that eventful occasion, will tell you the story of the battle of Pilot Knob in detail. Pages could be written on this subject. I repeat, the battle of Pilot Knob was one of the greatest battles of the civil war, because it marked the turning point of the war in Missouri, and in the trans-Mississippi country, and forever fixed the destiny of Missouri with respect to her position on the question of secession.

But, Mr. Chairman, it is cruel to expect these good people to remain standing longer in this rain, and I must bring my remarks to a close. (Cries of "Go on.") Were it not for the fact this is a non-political gathering, and I am a candidate, I'd like to tell you something concerning a bill which I introduced during the last session of Congress, and which is now pending before the committee on Military Affairs. (Col. Murphy, "You are at liberty to speak on any subject you desire, proceed"). Then Mr. Chairman, with your permission, I'll proceed briefly. The bill to which I refer seeks to create a National Military Park out of old Fort Davidson, and these sacred grounds. I failed to secure the passage of this bill for the reason, no bills were passed at the last session of Congress creating new sites for military parks. Some few appropriations, however, were made for the purpose of completing certain park improvements heretofore authorized, but no new sites were created. Hence, while I failed in my purpose, I fared no worse than others.

My colleague, Congressman Welbourn, of the Seventh district, introduced a bill which seeks to create a military park out of the old battlefield of Wilson's Creek. His bill, too, is pending before the committee. I am told by the chairman of the committee that at the coming session, our bills will be taken up. I believe this bill should pass for many reasons. It is the policy of our government to mark certain historic spots by statues and appropriate improvements. All over this country from Lakes to Gulf, and from sea to sea, we find on a hundred battlefields, statues, erected to the memory of some gallant hero, or to designate some great achievement. I shall ask the Congress to erect here, in old Fort Davidson, in Iron County, Missouri, a monument to the memory of those gallant heroes of ours, who gave their lives in the defense of the cause they believed to be just. I shall ask the Congress to do this, because in this fort, and on yonder hillside, fell as brave men as ever wore the gray and as loyal men as ever wore the blue. I shall ask the Congress to do this, because we already have a foothold near here at the Arcadia rifle range. Near here too, is the famous great oak and spring, where the invincible Grant received his commission as a Brigadier-General in the United States Army. I shall ask the Congress to pass my bill because Missouri is entitled to this recognition.

SURVIVORS OF THE BATTLE PRESENT, SEPTEMBER 27, 1906

Henry H. Ashbuagh	Starkdale, Mo.
Joseph W. Alexander	Farmington, Mo.
Isaac J. Bess	Doe Run, Mo.
John Blanks	Ironton, Mo.
C.C. Chandler	Bonne Terre, Mo.
Willis Cole	Ironton, Mo.
Isaac H. Dillon	Marling, Mo.
Herman Davis	Ironton, Mo.
Elijah Evans	Avon, Mo.
W.Z. Evans	Avon, Mo.
James Ellis	Pilot Knob, Mo.
David P. Floyd	Stockton, Mo.
Henry Fry	Doe Run, Mo.
Wm. A. Fletcher	Arcadia, Mo.
James Groves	Farmington, Mo.
Wm. T. Gay	Ironton, Mo.
Hardin Garner	St. Louis, Mo.
Peter Gerstenmeyer	Pilot Knob, Mo.

Robert Holland	Leeper, Mo.
John B. Hart	Doe Run, Mo.
Randolph James	Zalma, Mo.
Peter F. Kriminger	Doe Run, Mo.
Frederick Kaths	Pilot Knob, Mo.
Thomas Lang	Farmington, Mo.
Abram M. Lafferty	Middletown, Mo.
Solomon Lax	Ironton, Mo.
H.B. Milks	Leon, Kas.
David Murphy	St. Louis, Mo.
Wm. H. Musgrove	Flat River, Mo.
Azariah Martin	Ironton, Mo.
Wm. Nevin	Hahn, Mo.
John Newman	Ironton, Mo.
Thomas Newman	Ironton, Mo.
F.M. Parker	Coldwater, Mo.
John Parkin	Claytown, Mo.
Clark Powell	Sullivan Co., Mo.
Marvin P. Page	Mill Spring, Mo.
John W. Perry	North Alton, Ill.
Samuel Rhodes	Glen Allen, Mo.
Geo. W. Rhodes	Shrum, Mo.
C.C. Rust	Ironton, Mo.
B.B. Reagan	Ironton, Mo.
Alfred Shell	Hahn, Mo.
John O. Smith	Fredericktown, Mo.
John Schwab	Ironton, Mo.
Johnson M. Shell	Lutesville, Mo.
Ferd. O. Tennyson	Elvins, Mo.
Thos. J. Thompson	Higdon, Mo.
Henry Valle	Ironton, Mo.
Henry C. Wilkinson	Piedmont, Mo.
Joseph Wood	Mine La Motte, Mo.
Joel K.P. Wood	Irondale, Mo.
James H. White	Brunot, Mo.
W.M. Wilson	Arcadia, Mo.
Benj. Woodruff	Hendrickson, Mo.
Martin Wolf	Pilot Knob, Mo.
James Young	Bernie, Mo.

NECROLOGY

The following survivors of the battle of Pilot Knob have died in the past year:

JOHN K. BOWMAN
  Sergt. Co. L, 2d M.S.M. Cav., at Clarence, Mo., October 28, 1905.
JOHN L. BENNETT
  Private Co. G, 47th Mo. Inf., at Piedmont, Mo., February 16, 1906.
WM. T. MUDD
  Private, Co. D, 3rd M.S.M. Cav., at New Hartford, Mo., July 6, 1906.
SAMUEL GARDNER
  Private Co. F, 47th Mo. Inf., at Pittsburg, Kan., August 7, 1906.
WM. H. BURMINGHAM
  Private Co. A, 47th Mo. Inf., at Greenville, Mo., August 11, 1906.
SETH WINKLEPLECK
  Private Co. B, 14th Iowa Inf., at Waverly, Iowa, August 23, 1906.
THOS. T. DALTON
  Citizen defender, at Farmington, Mo., September 12, 1906.
JOSEPH A. BENNETT
  Private Co. A, 47th Mo. Inf., at Lodi, Mo., September 28, 1906.

APPENDIX

The following discussion of the Confederate and Union losses at the battle of Pilot Knob occurred in the latter part of the year 1905, and was conducted through a correspondence in the columns of the local newspapers published at Ironton, Mo.:

GEN. PRICE'S RAID.
IRONTON REGISTER, OCT. 12TH, 1905.

Editor Register: As I have seen so much written concerning the battle of Pilot Knob, and concerning General Price and his forces, I feel it is my duty to my comrades and the cause in which I was enlisted to write something.

I do not think General Price entered the State of Missouri with more than ten or fifteen thousand men, cavalry and artillery, and no infantry at all. If General Price had any serious intentions of going to St. Louis, he could not have changed his plans by the weakening of his forces at Pilot Knob. His losses were not over four hundred, killed, wounded and missing, and a portion of them were conscripts, who took advantage of the moment and skipped for Arkansas.

The morning after the battle I was left with my company in the rear to visit the fort and see if the dead had been collected. The men gathering the dead told me they had found about all the dead bodies, of which I counted forty-seven men, very near, if not all, of Cable's [sic] brigade of Arkansas troops. I took them to be his men from their uniforms, as they wore the gray, and the rest of the men wore mixed clothing; among the lot was the arm of a negro. I do not think the loss of the Union forces was very heavy. They must have taken their dead and wounded with them.

I think that General Price accomplished that which he intended to accomplish when entering the State of Missouri, that of recruiting his army. When he went out of the State into Kansas they issued rations for thirty-five thousand men, while he did not have more than ten thousand armed and fighting men.

I know there is a great deal of difference in this and what has been written concerning Price's raid and Pilot Knob battle; but believe they are as near the facts as can be given. While the Union forces defended the fort well, we had many harder fights on Price's raid than the battle of Pilot Knob.

C.K. Polk.

Col. Murphy Replies to Mr. Polk.
Arcadia Valley Enterprise, Oct. 20th, 1905.

Editor of the Enterprise: A friend has sent me a clipping from the *Register* of the 12th inst., which purports to be a letter from C.K. Polk, an ex-Confederate soldier, treating of the Price raid and the battle of Pilot Knob, and as some of the assertions contained in Mr. Polk's letter are so wide from established facts as to arouse a sense of surprise, I beg a little of your space wherein to reply.

Mr. Polk says: "I do not think General Price entered the State of Missouri with more than ten thousand or fifteen thousand men, cavalry and artillery."

General Price's official report of his raid shows that he entered Missouri with three divisions made up of nine brigades. In this army were thirty-three regiments, ten battalions, four batteries and one section of another battery, besides independent companies.

The regimental reports which have survived, and are still extant, show that their average strength was more than five hundred men to each regiment. The battalion strength is shown to have been nearly three hundred men to each organization, and the batteries and independent companies probably contained in the aggregate five hundred men.

This would make 21,000 men in Price's army at the lowest conservative estimate, which more probably contained 30,000 men, for Mr. Polk says: "When he (Price) went out of the State into Kansas they issued rations for 35,000 men," and General Price's report shows that he gathered 5,000 recruits in Missouri. Price's strength may have been as high as 35,000 men when he entered the State, for desertions were numerous all the way across the State, and it was estimated at the time of the raid that fully 1,000 deserted immediately after the battle of Pilot Knob.

Mr. Polk further says: "If General Price had any serious intention of going to St. Louis he could not have changed his plans by the weakening of his forces at Pilot Knob."

Let us appeal to the Official Records of the War of the Rebellion and see just what was Price's objective point. On August 4th, 1864, General E. Kirby Smith, commanding the Confederate Trans-Mississippi department, with headquarters at Shreveport, La., gave the order to General Price to invade Missouri, and used this language: "Make St. Louis the objective point of your movement, which if rapidly made, will put you in possession of that place, its supplies, and military stores, which will do more toward rallying Missouri to your standard than the possession of any other point." This should be sufficient to settle the point of Price's intended destination when he entered the State, but by way of corroboration we may quote General Joseph O. Shelby, who was in a position at that time to know what was going on. In a letter written to Major C.C. Rainwater as late as January 5th, 1888, General Shelby was discussing the failure of Price's movement into Missouri and described the council of war held at Fredericktown on September 25th, 1864. The question before the council was whether the army should move directly on St. Louis or go by way of Pilot Knob and capture the small garrison there so as to leave no enemy in the rear. Shelby voted to move on St. Louis and Fagan and Marmaduke voted to go by way of Pilot Knob and reduce that place, and this vote practically decided the fate of the Price raid, and almost the fate of Price's army. Describing this conference, Shelby says: "I favored moving rapidly into St. Louis and seizing it. I then and there stated what the result would be if we attacked Pilot Knob. I knew too well that good infantry well entrenched would give us h--l and h--l we did get!"

Mr. Polk, continuing, speaks of Price's losses at Pilot Knob and says: "His losses were not over four hundred, killed, wounded and missing, and a portion of them were conscripts who took advantage of the moment and skipped for Arkansas. The morning after the battle I was left with my company in the rear to visit the fort and see if the dead had been collected. The men gathering the dead told me they had found about all the dead bodies, of which I counted forty-seven men, very near, if not all, of Cabble's (Cabell's) brigade of Arkansas troops."

This is a most astounding assertion, and I shall quote some Confederate authorities on the subject. A Confederate from the ranks who participated in the battle of Pilot Knob has written his recollections of the engagement, and in describing the scene as he rode over the battlefield the next morning says: "We passed many poor fellows lying cold and stark in death, to-day, who in the prime of life were the choice of the van yesterday. I do no know how many were killed and wounded on our side, but we estimated 150 to 200 killed and 200 to 300 wounded." This was the opinion of an honest man, telling an honest story of what he saw before the dead were collected.

In a recent conversation with Colonel John P. Bull, of St. Louis, who led his Confederate Arkansas regiment in the assault on Fort Davidson on September 27th, 1864, he told me that he left 42 of his regiment dead and mortally wounded on the field. As there were 27 regiments, 8 battalions and 4 batteries engaged in the battle on the Confederate side the fair minded man of to-day can do some honest computing on his own account as to what the Confederate loss probably was, if one regiment lost 42 men by death. But we also find something of an official, or semi-official, character from that side worthy of noting. General Price studiously suppressed the figures of his losses in this battle, in his official report, but in 1894 Captain T.J. Mackey wrote an account of the battle. He had been chief engineer on Price's staff and was in the fight. He knew much of the details of the battle and had access to the official information accumulated. In his story of the battle he does not mention the total number of killed and wounded, but in describing the disastrous results of the assault on the fort he says: "In fifteen minutes we lost 1,056 men killed and wounded." And this does not include the hundreds killed and wounded on September 26th and 27th before the assault, nor those killed and wounded after the assault.

Now for a few statistics accumulated after the battle:

Dr. T.W. Johnson, in charge of our post hospital, remained behind with our wounded, when we retired, and spent some time on the battlefield and in the Confederate hospitals at Ironton. In his official report he states that when he last talked with the Confederate non-commissioned officer in charge of their burial squads, the latter showed him his list, and there had then been 335 buried on the battlefield, and the scattered dead on the mountains had not been collected. These are known to have amounted to about 75 killed. The Confederates admitted to Dr. Johnson that their loss was 400 killed and a corresponding number wounded, which would make their total losses in killed and wounded anywhere from 1,600 to 2,400.

Captain M.D. Smith was one of the first Union officers to return to Pilot Knob, and he interviewed Colonel Wyatt C. Thomas, General Fagan's chief of staff, in the hospital at Ironton, and on asking him what the Confederate losses were reports his reply as follows: "His reply was that they lost 1,500, and that of the best men they had; that he was wounded in the last charge on the fort and had as good an opportunity of knowing their loss as any man engaged. He also spoke of the recklessness and bravery of our men; that the determination and bravery displayed by them had never been equaled."

Major H.H. Williams, of the 10th Kansas Volunteers, was also located at Pilot Knob after the battle, and after prosecuting diligent inquiry among the Confederate wounded in hospital and citizens who witnessed the battle and the burial of the dead, he found no estimate of the Confederate losses in killed and wounded, from any source, below 1,500, while many of the estimates exceeded 2,000.

Lieutenant Colonel A.W. Maupin, of the 47th Missouri Infantry, was also stationed at Pilot Knob soon after the raid, and he, too, took pains to compile all available data from wounded Confederates, and from citizens, and the lowest estimate he could figure from these, of Confederate losses, was 1,525 killed and wounded.

So it would seem that Mr. Polk is a gentleman of very limited powers of observation, else he could not have committed himself to making such a statement as purports to have come from him. As an index to his faculty of acquiring information, I must again quote from his letter where he touches upon the Union losses and the disposition of their dead and wounded. "They must have taken their dead and wounded with them!" For forty-one years it has been a fact as well known in Arcadia Valley as that a battle was fought there, that the Union dead were buried in graves singly, or covered by the explosion of the magazine, and that fifty odd wounded were carried to the local hospital, where they were left under the care of Doctors S.D. Carpenter and T.W. Johnson. Several of Mr. Polk's neighbors served as nurses in this hospital, and many others still living near him know the facts. From this I fear that Mr. Polk has not been an eager inquirer after facts during his residence in Southeast Missouri since the close of the Civil War.

David Murphy.
St. Louis, Oct. 19th, 1905.

*Col. Murphy's article was also sent to the *Register*, but was not inserted then for lack of space.—Ed.

MR. POLK'S REJOINDER
IRONTON REGISTER, NOV. 23RD, 1905.

Editor Register: I noticed a few weeks ago in the local columns of your paper that Colonel Murphy would have an article the next week concerning the battle of Pilot Knob. It seems, for some cause, he chose the *Arcadia Valley Enterprise**. Will you kindly give me space to reply to his article. Colonel Murphy says some of the assertions in my letter are "so wide from established facts as to arouse a sense of surprise." I will just say it was the wide difference between the published so-called facts that caused my reply to J.E.M.'s article taken from the Fredericktown paper.

Colonel Murphy starts out by quoting General Price's official report of entering the State, showing that General Price had three divisions, made of nine brigades. He says "in this army were 33 regiments of more than 500 men to the regiment, and 10 battalions. His battalion strength shows to have been nearly 300 men; this would make 2,100 [*sic*] men in Price's army, which more probably contained 30,000 men." Here you see that Colonel Murphy denies General Price's report and quotes myself as authority, from the fact that I stated in my article that when he went out of the State into Kansas he issued rations for 35,000 men. It is not necessary to further discuss General Price's intention for entering the State. We will confine ourselves to the facts of the battle of Pilot Knob.

Colonel Murphy says my statement in regard to the killed and wounded "is a most astounding assertion," and that he would quote some Confederate authority on the subject: "A Confederate from the ranks who participated in the battle of Pilot Knob has written his recollections of the engagement, and in describing the scene as he rode over the battlefield the next morning, says: 'We estimated our losses 150 to 200 killed and 200 to 300 wounded;'" which would make 350 killed at lowest estimate, and 500 at highest; so the Colonel will see from this quoted authority that he has 500 killed, and not the 1,600 or 2,400, as he quoted in his article. "This is the opinion of an honest man telling an honest story of what he saw before the dead were collected." The Colonel seems to insinuate here that I am not an honest man, or telling an honest story, and that the man who rode over the battlefield could give a more correct report than the man who counted the dead. Of course, Colonel Murphy did not think this; he must have been somewhat excited to know that a Confederate is still living who knew the facts as they existed at the battle of Pilot Knob. Colonel Murphy says that Colonel John P. Bull stated to him that he left 42 of his dead and wounded on the field. I stated in my article that the 47 men were nearly all Arkansas troops.

149

Colonel Murphy says there were 27 regiments and 8 battalions on the Confederate side, and indicates that 42 men were lost to each regiment. Now, Colonel, I did not, in my limited powers of observation, only count the men, but I saw them fall in the battle, and this is the loss in dead in the assault by the Arkansas troops. They were the only troops that ever reached the ditch of the fort. No other command could have sustained as great a loss.

The Colonel says: "But we also find something of an official or semi-official character from that side worthy of noting. General Price studiously suppressed the figures of his losses in this battle in his official report." In referring to Dr. J.W. [sic] Johnson, in charge of the Union hospital, talking with a Confederate non-commissioned officer of the burial squad, the latter showed him his list, and there had been 335 buried on the battlefield, and the scattered men on the mountains had not been collected, "which was known to amount to 75 men." Here we see the Colonel has 410 killed. He further quoted Dr. Johnson, saying: "Their loss was 400 killed and a corresponding number wounded," which we understand to be 800 killed and wounded. The Colonel says: "This would make their losses in killed and wounded anywhere from 1,600 to 2,400." He acknowledges that there were some men killed in the fort, buried in single graves and covered by the magazine explosion. Now the Colonel has been telling the number that were killed on the Confederate side; if he sees fit, will he please give us an account of the dead and wounded on the Union side?

C.K. Polk.

COL. MURPHY'S FINAL STATEMENT.
ARCADIA VALLEY ENTERPRISE. DEC. 28TH, 1905.

Editor Gibbs: My attention has been called to another contribution from C.K. Polk in the columns of the *Register* of Nov. 23rd, regarding the battle of Pilot Knob, and as Mr. Polk has surrendered his opinion on one vital point set up in his first letter, viz: Price's destination on coming into Missouri, I will now offer some additional authorities on the matter of losses in the battle.

Let me first recapitulate what I offered in my previous letter as the accepted foundation for statistics of Confederate killed and wounded, all of which Mr. Polk brushes aside as so much chaff.

A Confederate enlisted man riding along the road through the battlefield, saw sufficient before there dead were collected to estimate their dead at 150 to 200 and their wounded at 200 to 300. Colonel John P. Bull lost 42 from his Arkansas regiment by death. Captain T.J. Mackey of Price's staff says they lost 1,056 men killed and wounded in fifteen minutes during the charge. Colonel

Wyatt C. Thomas of Fagan's staff, in conversation with numerous Union officers, placed their loss at 1,500. These are all Confederate authorities.

Of Union authorities I quoted Captain Marcus D. Smith, Major H.H. Williams, Lieutenant Colonel A.W. Maupin and Dr. T.W. Johnson, each of which made separate and independent investigations and inquiries, and all placed the Confederate loss at 1,500 or over.

But this does not satisfy Mr. Polk. He was there and saw them killed and counted them. There were just 47 killed and it was his duty to see that they were collected for burial, for he and his company had been detailed to do this. Now I beg to introduce another count of the dead made on the field early in the morning of September 28th, before the Confederates had arrived or began collecting their dead. Dr. S.D. Carpenter left the Union hospital in Pilot Knob that morning while the field was wholly unoccupied, except by dead and wounded, and going out to the fort, stood on its wall and counted 67 dead lying near the ditch. This fact is recorded along with his account of the battle on October 5, 1864, not after memory had played its pranks for forty-one years.

But I will quote some additional Confederate authorities. The secession Governor of Missouri, Thos. C. Reynolds, was with Price at the battle of Pilot Knob, and in December, 1864, wrote his account of the raid, and speaking of the failure to capture Fort Davidson, he says: "He (Price) lost several hundred of his best soldiers in the repulsed attempt to storm the well ditched fort at Pilot Knob." Mind you now, not 47 men, but several hundred. Several is a very flexible adjective and may mean anywhere from three hundred to seven hundred or eight hundred, and they were lost in the repulsed assault on the fort.

Mr. Polk objects to taking the mortalities (42) men in Colonel Bull's Arkansas regiment as a basis for computing the Confederate losses, and states that the Arkansas troops were the only ones that reached the ditch. There were 16 regiments and four battalions in Fagan's division, all being Arkansas troops, except one Missouri regiment, and it was this division that charged up to the ditch. The law of averages can be applied to as many of these regimental and battalion organizations as Mr. Polk desires, or he can cut them all out except Bull's regiment, if that suits his purpose better. Persons, however, who wish to arrive at a fair conclusion will probably include the whole division in their estimate. I wish to deal absolutely fair with Mr. Polk. He claims to have witnessed this fruitless sacrifice of the Arkansas troops, but does not claim to have taken an active part in the assault on the fort. He probably belonged to Marmaduke's division, which was made up of seven

Missouri regiments, two Missouri battalions and one Arkansas battalion, while Slayback's Missouri battalion from Shelby's division was temporarily attached or co-operating during the engagement. The official Confederate reports of the battle all yield the point that discretion was considered the better part of valor in this division when it came to making the assault on Fort Davidson. Mr. Polk practically says that none of this division reached the ditch, and the writer, who was an interested eye-witness to the event, is prepared to subscribe to the correctness of his assertion. The Confederate reports show that two regiments of this division, Burbridge's 4th Missouri Cavalry and Jeffer's 8th Missouri Cavalry, never got any nearer to the fort than the dry bed of Stouts Creek, where they laid down in a place of comparative security until nightfall. But Colonel Burbridge made a report of his losses in the battle, "seven officers and 28 men killed and wounded." This is the loss of a regiment which admittedly and notoriously had less to do with the battle than any other regiment or battalion in that division, engaged in the fight, except Jeffer's regiment. Mr. Polk will certainly admit that Burbridge's loss of 35 killed and wounded is not an unfair ratio to apply to Marmaduke;'s whole division of seven regiments and four battalions, and this would show a loss of 329 killed and wounded in this division, which did not charge the fort. It is a well known fact that Marmaduke's right, which kept in touch with Fagan's left suffered much more severely than the left wing did, where Burbridge and Jeffers concealed their regiments in the dry bed of the creek.

After the Confederates had gathered and buried their dead (and Mr. Polk claims to have been one of those left behind to see that it was well and properly done) at least 75 dead were found abandoned to the prey of hogs and dogs roaming over the battlefield. Most of these were along Stout's Creek and up the slope of Shepherd Mountain to its very top, 1,200 yards distant from the fort. At one spot, in the ravine on the northeast slope of the mountain, 16 bodies were found two weeks later within a few feet of each other, and buried by the Union burial detail.

There were four Confederate batteries in the engagement and their losses have not been considered in the foregoing, but each battery certainly lost some men. As late as October 12, 1864, there were representatives of all four batteries still in the hospital at Ironton among the mortally or seriously wounded. Mr. Thomas Newman, now, as then, a resident of Ironton, has related how he and his brother were held prisoners during the battle on top of Shepherd Mountain and they saw a shell from the fort strike and explode immediately at the Confederate gun, disabling the piece and killing or seriously wounding about a dozen men. And this was 1,200 yards from the fort and the most remote point at which any of Price's guns were placed.

Mr. Polk seems to be inclined to quibble with my figures when I used the expression "400 killed and a corresponding number wounded," in my previous letter. The number of wounded corresponding to the killed in the various battles of the Civil War, ran from three wounded to one killed in short range engagements, up to six wounded to one killed in long range. The average for the whole war was 480 wounded to each 100 killed. At Gettysburg the fighting was at all ranges and the ratio was 470 wounded to 100 killed. The battle of Pilot Knob was much like Gettysburg in its characteristics, being fought at all ranges of firearms and terminating in a disastrous repulsed assault, and if we apply this average to General Price's losses we will have 400 killed (minimum estimate) and 1,880 wounded. Applying the law of averages as established by the Civil War mortuary statistics, i.e., 64 mortally wounded to each 100 killed, we would have 265 mortally wounded to add to the 400 killed in Price's army on September 26 and 27, 1864. On this point General Thomas Ewing may be quoted. He visited the Confederate hospital at Ironton on October 12, 1864, and reported that he found there: "One colonel, three majors, seven captains, twelve lieutenants and 204 enlisted men representing seventeen regiments and four batteries, all dangerously and nearly all mortally wounded." A total of 227 men in this condition more than two weeks after the battle. At that time an open burying trench was kept by the hospital, and the wounded were dying at the rate of five to eight per day. Let us apply the law of averages once more. Where careful statistics were kept following great battles during the Civil War, it was found that three-fourths of the mortally wounded died inside of a week, and yet this condition and these numbers were found at Ironton at the end of two weeks or more. General Price, before leaving Pilot Knob, had ordered all the wounded who could probably stand transportation to be moved south, and this was done by an improvised ambulance train under escort of Colonel Rains' regiment.

Now a few words about the Union losses at Pilot Knob, which Mr. Polk asks for. The name of every man who perished in that battle under the Stars and Strips has been sacredly preserved, and shall some day appear in imperishable bronze on the battlefield. We have nothing to conceal and have always courted the fullest publicity. There were 14 killed, 14 mortally wounded and 44 surviving wounded as a total casualty list in General Ewing's little band. Of the mortally wounded, eight died inside of three days after the battle. Mr. Polk is entitled to record his count, but it will never change the facts and figures which have gone into history. Whether he arrived on the ground after all the collected dead were buried except 47, or whether his count was only as accurate as his observance of orders to see all the dead collected, I shall not attempt to decide.

In conclusion it is desired to remind Mr. Polk that he has placed a lower estimate on the valor and stamina of the Confederate soldier than any other person who has ever attempted to throw a sidelight on the battle of Pilot Knob. The writer has witnessed what kind of impetuous bravery inspired the mistaken heroes in the Southern army at Wilson's Creek, Prairie Grove, Vicksburg, Pilot Knob and other fields of honor and strife, and knows what kind of punishment they were always ready to take before acknowledging defeat, and when it is intimated that an army as large as Price's retired discomfited before Ewing's little band after having lost only 47 men, less than one company out of more than 300 companies, it is so gross a reflection on the gallantry of the Confederate soldier that it should not be permitted to pass without rebuke from the survivors of the battle on that side.

David Murphy.
St. Louis, Mo., Dec. 8th, 1905.

On the back cover of the booklet was the following information:

The Pilot Knob Memorial Association is supported entirely by voluntary contributions from survivors of the battle, their friends and others patriotically inclined. The following contributions have been received since our second annual meeting in 1905:

David Murphy, St. Louis, Mo.	$10.00
H.C. Townsend, St. Louis, Mo.	2.00
Isaac H. Dillon, Marling, Mo.	2.00
James M. Ross, Fulton, Ill	.2.00
Hugo Hoffbuaer, Buffalo, Ia.	2.00
W.C. Breckenridge, St. Louis, Mo.	1.00
W.F. Parks, St. Louis, Mo.	1.00
W.V. Lucas, Santa Cruz, Cal.	1.00
W.H. Cameron, Warrenton, Mo.	1.00
Peter Shrum, Sligo, Mo.	.75
Henry Anderson, Hickman, Ky.	.60
Total, $23.35	

A deficit of more than $100 exists in our printing and postage account, and this is being carried by a member of the Association. Contributions to this account and the battlefield purchase fund will be properly credited if sent to

C.A. Peterson, Cor. Sec'y.,
Box 980 St. Louis, Mo.

On the back page of the booklet was information regarding an Iron Mountain railroad route leading to the "Famous Pilot Knob Battlefield" and to "Beautiful Arcadia Valley," which were reached by the "St. Louis, Iron Mountain & Southern Ry" via six trains daily in each direction.

Appendix 1

Troops Known to Have Been in the Arcadia Valley during the Civil War

1861

Stewart's Independent (Illinois) Cavalry Company

1st Illinois Light Artillery Volunteers, Batteries A and B

7th Illinois Infantry Volunteers

17th Illinois Infantry Volunteers, Colonel L.F. Ross

19th Illinois Infantry Volunteers, Colonel J.B. Turchin

20th Illinois Infantry Volunteers

21st Illinois Infantry Volunteers, Colonel U.S. Grant, Lieutenant Colonel Alexander

24th Illinois Infantry Volunteers, Colonel Franz Hecker

33rd Illinois Infantry Volunteers, Colonel C.E. Hovey

38th Illinois Infantry Volunteers, Colonel W.P. Carlin

1st Indiana Cavalry Volunteers, Colonel Conrad Baker

2nd Iowa Infantry Volunteers

7th Iowa Infantry Volunteers

Benton (Missouri) Hussars Cavalry Battalion

Simpson's Regiment (Missouri) State Militia Infantry

1st Missouri Light Artillery, Battery A, Major John M. Schofield, and Battery H, Captain Francis H. Manter

2nd Missouri Infantry Volunteers, Colonel Fred Schaefer

4th Missouri Volunteers [U.S. Reserve Corps] Colonel B. Gratz Brown

6th Missouri Infantry Volunteers, Colonel P.E. Bland

24th Missouri Infantry, Colonel Sempronius H. Boyd

Hawkin's Missouri Independent Cavalry, Captain Hawkin

Major Garitt's Ind [Indiana or Independent?] Cavalry

Pilot Knob Home Guard (Schmitz's Independent Company), Captain Ferdinand Schmitz

1st Nebraska Infantry Volunteers, Colonel J.M. Thayer

8th Wisconsin Infantry Volunteers (Eagle Regiment)

One section of Engineer Corps (Pioneers), Captain William Hoelcke

Battery of four guns, Captain F. McMasters

1862

2nd Arkansas Cavalry Volunteers

Dodson's Kane County (Illinois) Independent Company Cavalry

2nd Illinois Light Artillery Volunteers, Battery A

5th Illinois Cavalry Volunteers

9th Illinois Cavalry Volunteers

13th Illinois Cavalry Volunteers, Colonel Jos. [Joseph] Bell

33rd Illinois Infantry Volunteers

38th Illinois Infantry Volunteers

8th Indiana Infantry Volunteers

23rd Iowa Infantry Volunteers

50th Indiana Infantry Volunteers

3rd Iowa Cavalry Volunteers

Simpson's Regiment (Missouri) State Militia Infantry

Welfley's Independent (Missouri) Battery Light Artillery

1st Missouri State Militia Infantry, Colonel John B. Grey

1st Missouri Light Artillery Volunteers

2nd Missouri Light Artillery Volunteers, Battery A

3rd Missouri Infantry

3rd Missouri Cavalry Volunteers

4th Missouri Cavalry Volunteers

5th Missouri Cavalry (Major General Sigel's Bodyguards, Second Lieutenant J. Montzheimer)

6th Missouri Cavalry, Company F

12th Missouri State Militia Cavalry, Colonel Albert Jackson

17th Missouri Infantry Volunteers

24th Missouri Infantry Volunteers

68th Enrolled Missouri Militia (Haw Eaters), Colonel James Lindsay
1st Nebraska Infantry Volunteers
4th Ohio Independent Battery Light Artillery
16th Ohio Independent Battery Light Artillery
1st Wisconsin Cavalry Volunteers
11th Wisconsin Infantry Volunteers

1863

2nd Division Army of the Frontier
3rd Colorado Cavalry (formerly 3rd Colorado Infantry)
2nd Illinois Light Artillery, Battery A, "Peoria Battery" Volunteers
10th Illinois Cavalry Volunteers
13th Illinois Cavalry Volunteers, Colonel A.A. Gorgas
99th Illinois Infantry Volunteers (at Middlebrook) Colonel G.W.K. Bailey
1st Indiana Independent Battery Light Artillery
8th Indiana Infantry Volunteers
18th Indiana Infantry Volunteers
26th Indiana Infantry Volunteers
1st Iowa Infantry Volunteers
3rd Iowa Cavalry Volunteer
20th Iowa Infantry Volunteers
21st Iowa Infantry Volunteers (at Iron Mountain)
22nd Iowa Infantry Volunteers (at Iron Mountain)
23rd Iowa Infantry Volunteers (at Iron Mountain)
34th Iowa Infantry Volunteers
1st Missouri State Militia Infantry, Colonel John B. Grey, Colonel John F. Tyler
1st Missouri Light Artillery Volunteers
1st Missouri Cavalry Volunteers
2nd Missouri Light Artillery Volunteers, Batteries D, K and M
2nd Missouri Cavalry (Merrill's Horse) Volunteers
2nd Missouri State Militia Cavalry
3rd Missouri Cavalry Volunteers
3rd Missouri State Militia Cavalry, Colonel Robert Woodson
4th Missouri Cavalry Volunteers
7th Missouri Cavalry Volunteers
8th Missouri Cavalry Volunteers

8th Provisional Enrolled Missouri Militia (68th Enrolled Missouri Militia)

10th Missouri State Militia Cavalry, Colonel Edwin Smart

24th Missouri Infantry Volunteers

25th Missouri Infantry Volunteers

1st Nebraska Cavalry (formerly 1st Nebraska Infantry)

25th Ohio Independent Battery, Light Artillery

1st Wisconsin Cavalry

11th Wisconsin Infantry Volunteers

1864

135th Illinois Infantry Volunteers, Colonel John S. Wolfe

14th Iowa Infantry Volunteers, Captain William Campbell

10th Kansas Volunteers Cavalry, Major H.H. Williams

1st Missouri State Militia Infantry

2nd Missouri State Militia Cavalry (one company)

2nd Missouri Light Artillery, Batteries G and H

3rd Missouri State Militia Cavalry

6th Missouri Cavalry Volunteers (4 companies)

6th Missouri State Militia Cavalry

47th Missouri Infantry Volunteers, Colonel A.W. Maupin

50th Missouri Infantry Volunteers, Colonel David Murphy

St. Louis and Iron Mountain Railroad Enrolled Missouri Militia, General Madison Miller

1865

17th Illinois Cavalry, Colonel John L. Beveridge, Captain Jesse D. Butts

7th Kansas Cavalry Volunteers (Jayhawkers), Lieutenant Colonel Francis Malone

10th Kansas Volunteer Cavalry, Major H.H. Williams

2nd Missouri State Militia Cavalry

50th Missouri Volunteer Infantry, Colonel David Murphy

51st Missouri Volunteer Infantry, Company D

Work compiled by Jack Mayes, Joe Snyder and Walter Busch.

Appendix 2

Text for Selected Photos

VIEW OF THE ARMORED PLAN OF FORT DAVIDSON AT PILOT KNOB, MISSOURI

Picture and notes on page 47.
View of the Armored Plan of Fort Davidson at Pilot Knob, Mo., as surveyed and drawn by Sergt. Henry C. Wilkinson, one of the participants at the Battle of Pilot Knob, Mo., Sept. 27, 1864, 10:35 A.M., to 2 P.M., as photoed by J. Siler of 1006 S. 7th St., St. Louis, Mo., by permission of Sergt. Wilkinson, the original designer, surveyor of Wayne Co., Mo.—This is conceded to be the finest designed and reproduced plan of a fort ever presented to the public—it is of great value to the survivors of this battle, which never was officially reported by its commandant officer, Gen. Thos. Ewing, Jr. The peculiar pressing circumstances attending this battle—the shrewd evacuation of the fort—saving a ton of ammunition by Private W.H. Moore, Co. H, 3rd Regt. Mo. S.M., at 1:20 A.M. of Sept. 28, he rejoining Capt. H.B. Milks and the 20 men, helped to save that powder—the retreat so well covered by Capt. Wm. J. Campbell to Leasburg, thence to Rolla, Mo., 120 m., were certainly exciting events—no report of battle was made.—The Photographer having lost the photo items furnished by his friends, Dr. C.A. Peterson, Cor. Sec. of the Pilot Knob Memorial Association, as well as those forwarded by Sergt. Hy. C. Wilkinson, cannot describe the fort's cannon's positions. There is absolutely no time to get duplicates of those photo items lost, as this book must be

out for the Reunion.—The 13 cannon mounted in the fort during the battle are shown in their correct positions—field piece 18 at the E. end of the drawbridge was brought into the fort by Sergt. Wilkinson and his volunteer squad, who sallied over the drawbridge and recovered the gun—the enemy wanted it, too, 7 is where Private W.H. Moore came out the last man from the magazine, having fixed that dry powder to his tow-string—the powder was saved—the Confederates awoke to find a bright noise a la 4th of July on—and the Union boys in blue vanishing from sight n.w. on Belleview road, on to Leasburg, thence to Rolla.

All survivors buying a copy of this book will confer a favor by forwarding their full names, the Co. and Regt. they belonged to, and the number of their picture as shown in the survivors' group photo shown in this book, and their present address, and give the names and numbers of the comrades shown in this photo book, that the photographer may publish a special description of this fort, guns and participants shown in the survivor's group. Please use pen and ink in answering this request.

Handwritten notes around photos and text:

1. Crest of Parapets
2. Moat or Ditch 10 feet deep.
3. Steps to firing platform.
4. Gateway and drawbridge.
5. Sally Port of Covered Way.
6. Magazine like a huge dirt cellar.
7. Entrance to Magazine.
8. Posts and windlasses to draw up the Bridge.
9. Portion of North rifle pit 196 yards long.
10. South rifle pit extending to Stout's [Knob] Creek 156 yards.
11. (See printed explanation.)
12. 32 pounder siege guns.
12A. Dismounted in action.
12B. Gun that opened the Battle at 9 to 9.15 A.M. Sept. 27[th] '64. Also, this gun at second shot aim by Lieutenant Jno. Fessler dislo[d]ged the Rebel battery on Shepherd's Mt. crest at about 2.45 P.M. Sept 27[th] '64 at 800 yards.
13. 24 pounder howitzers.
13A. Howitzer that riddled the "Knob Store" at 10 A.M. (See holes in ware house).
14. 3 inch or 12 pounder rifled steel field guns. Battery H 2nd Mo. Light Art.
15. Cohorn mortars line of 24 howitzers.

16. Rebels driven back with hand grenades by Capt. Wm. J. Campbell, comdng 14th Iowa Inft.

17. Rebel line closing in but driven back with dreadful loss.

18. A field gun that failed to get into the fort time of the assault. Brought in by Damon J. Taylor of Co. G 47th Mo. Inft. Vols., and other volunteers. (Correction. Sergt. H.C. Wilkinson & others covered this gun from the gate way which had fallen back but did not participate in the bringing in of the gun. He saw the sallying party come in with this gun, but had been called back to south parapet at the time. H.C.W.)

Of gun at 18. It was unlimbered where it stood until the enemy was driven back. The gun team became unruly and the gun was unlimbered in order to save it. D.J.

Taylor states that the outer end of the draw bridge had not sunk back to its level and the first attempt to bring in the gun failed. Then they backed her off and placed incline boards so as to bring the wheels onto the drawbridge and into the fort. He says "Murphy said 'Now boys run her up, and give 'em h__l with her!' which they did." D.J. Taylor belonged to Co. G 47th Mo. Inft. Vols but was assigned to the artillery during the battle and retreat to Leasburg.

19. At 19 there stood three guns not in use in the battle. They were very small light pieces 1 3/4 to 2 inch caliber. [Author's note: Colonel James Lindsay, Enrolled Missouri Militia, bought six Woodruff guns for his EMM, and they were kept at the fort. Out of the thirty-six known to have been assembled, five are known to still exist. The two at West Point came from the St. Louis Arsenal, and there is a good probability that they came from this fort.]

VIEW OF THE PILOT KNOB, MISSOURI BATTLEFIELD

Picture and notes on page 48.

As photoed by J. Siler of St. Louis, Mo., Aug. 5, 1906, 12:17 p.m., looking e. from s. slope of Cedar Mtn. observation rock, 300 ft. above the church shown in Photo A.—Shepherd Mtn. (1610 ft. high) is shown from S to I. At I & W is the Pilot Knob & Ironton wagon road gap, through which Gen. Sterling Price's Confederate army approached the plain 1/2 m. wide, in which Fort Davidson is located on 1 acre, shown at F, where the 9 inch diam. elm and sycamore trees have grown in and about the fort since the Battle of Pilot Knob, Mo., Sept. 27, 1864, 10:35 a.m.—The massed

columns led the great final assault 2 p.m.—At I was the first position of the Confederate battery. At C and the E slope of Shepherd Mtn. was the second position. Col. David Murphy, Chief of Artillery in the fort, personally aimed the fort cannon whose 2d shot hit the Confederate cannon (the enemy left) the C position.—There were 13 cannon in Fort Davidson, supported by 1000 infantry, shooting at close range, held the enemy off until night. Gen. Thos. Ewing, Jr., in command of the Union army at Pilot Knob. W is at the w. base of Pilot Knob Mtn. (is 1531 ft. high) is where Maj. Jas. Wilson was captured and was murdered by Price's Raiders. Oct. 3, 1864 in Franklin Co., Mo.—At the right L is where Capt. Wm. P.[J.] Campbell, with 14 Regt. Iowa, held the n.w. spur of Shepherd Mtn., but was forced back to the rifle pits at the fort from which the entire Union force retreated into the fort, including the field artillery, which was drawn in by hand. Capt. H.B. Milks secured all but one cannon. This was secured by Sergt. Hy. C. Wilkinson and several volunteers, who sallied from the fort and rescued the piece—the drawbridge hoisted, the Union army was cooped—but not captured.—The 10,000 Confederates made their great effort to capture the fort at 2 p.m. by a general assault—which failed—the Confederate loss was 400 killed, 175 mortally wounded and over 1000 wounded.—The Union or Federal army lost 15 killed, 11 mortally wounded, and 46 wounded.—Total deaths of both armies were 601; wounded 1045 men.—Fort Davidson was evacuated the night after the battle and was blown up at 1:30 a.m., Sept. 28th.—Capt. H.B. Milks was in charge of the party who prepared the fort's ammunition, by fuse lighted by Private W.H. Moore, Co. H, 3rd Regt. Mo. S.M.—he lit the prepared fuse and hurried from the fort, being the last man; retreated n.w. on the Belleview road, via the shortest roads to Leasburg, on Frisco Railway, to Cuba, on for Rolla, Mo.—Capt. Campbell commanded the protecting rear column of the Union army against the repeated assaults of Gen. Price's pursing columns of cavalry all day Sept. 28 and night and Sept. 29.—I am indebted to friend Dr. C.A. Peterson, Prest. Mo. Hist. Soc.; Corspdg. Sec. of the Pilot Knob Memorial Association, for cheerful assistance and valuable data herein utilized. I must not forget Capt. H.B. Milks, nor friend Sergt. Hy. C. Wilkinson, surveyor of Fort Davidson.
[Handwritten] X Wm. J. Campbell.

THE SURVIVORS OF THE BATTLE OF PILOT KNOB, MISSOURI, IN FORT DAVIDSON, FORTY-TWO YEARS AFTER THE BATTLE: THE SECOND REUNION

Picture and notes on page 53.

Photoed Sept. 27, 1905, 5:35 p.m., looking due E., showing the famous Pilot Knob mountain (is 1531 ft. above sea) at the left. Used as a signal station by Gen. Thos. Ewing, Jr., the union commandant in the fort, which occupied 1 acre.—Gen. Sterling Price was in command of the Confederate army, 10,000 strong. Fort Davidson is nearly in the same condition as 42 years ago, Sept. 29, 1864, 1:20 A.M., when Private W.H. Moore, Co. H, 3rd Regt. Mo. S.M., saved the powder of the fort—he hurried away—those elm trees 9 inches in diameter mark the hole of the fort magazine, and the well-frogs now garrison the fort. Pilot Knob Battle commenced 10:35 A.M., and the great general assault 2 P.M.—It failed.—The Confederate loss was 400 killed, 175 mortally wounded, 1000 slightly wounded.—The Union or Federal army in the fort was 1000 strong; its loss was 15 killed, 11 mortally wounded and 46 slightly wounded.—Here are the names of the Union survivors of this battle, shown in the photo as known to the photographer (as his list of names and photo items are lost): No. 1 is Major David Murphy, who was Chief of Artillery of the Union army. It was the Major then who personally sighted the cannon which quickly dislodged the Confederate battery on E. slope of Shepherd Mountain (is 1610 ft. above sea). See photo of battlefield at C. This precise, quick work discouraged the enemy throughout the battle. It was a strong factor to save the Union army.—4 is Sergt. Hy. C. Wilkinson, who with a volunteer squad sallied out of the drawbridge and brought in the field piece which the enemy wanted.—Mr. Wilkinson recently surveyed the fort and drew a fine map of the fort and the original positions of each of the 13 cannon. The photographer here tenders his thanks for the map, etc., drawn, of which photo is shown in this book. 2 is Mr. John S. Luthy, the drummer, whose continuous service in and about the fort is highly appreciated by all true blues.—Dr. C.A. Peterson, although too young to serve in 1861, is certainly making great efforts to serve the patriotic movement to perpetuate the memory of his brother, who fell in the Union ranks at Fredericktown, Mo., Oct. 21, 1861.—Dr. Peterson is now Cor. Sec. of the Pilot Knob Memorial Association and has continuously for 4 yrs. steadily advanced the interest of the Association. Dr. Peterson is not shown in the survivors' group.—The margin of this Photo is left for the survivors to write with pen and ink each other's names for future reference. As Old Glory was introduced in the last photo taken by friend W.C. Perkins, photographer at Ironton, Mo., I have used his photo, that Old Glory may be seen as of days of yore floating over its defenders.

Appendix 3

H.R. 4923: A Bill to Create Pilot Knob National Battlefield

From the Missouri Historical Society's Cyrus Peterson Collection, Box 9, Folder 4, Representative Politte Elvins' Letter, April 9, 1909.

A similar bill was introduced by the Honorable M. Rhodes in the 59th Congress. In his letter, Representative Elvins assures Dr. Peterson that upon the insertion of a few missing words he will introduce it during the sessions in 1909.

H.R. 4923
of the 60th Congress, 1st session.

IN THE HOUSE OF REPRESENTATIVES
December 5, 1909.
Mr. Smith, of Missouri, introduced the following bill; which was referred to the Committee on Military Affairs and ordered to be printed.

A BILL
To establish a national military park to commemorate the battle of Pilot Knob, Missouri.

Be it enacted by the Senate and House of Representatives of the United States of America in Congress assembled, That in order to commemorate the battle of Pilot Knob and to preserve the history of the events which occurred during the last invasion of Missouri in eighteen hundred and sixty-four and in said battle, the battlefield of Pilot Knob, in the State of Missouri, is hereby declared to be a national military park whenever the title to same shall have been acquired by the United States and the usual jurisdiction over the lands and roads of the same shall have been granted to the United States by the State of Missouri; that is to say, the area inclosed in lots numbered fifty, fifty-one, fifty-two, fifty-four, fifty-five, fifty-six, fifty-seven, fifty-eight, fifty-nine, sixty, sixty-one, sixty-two, sixty-three, sixty-four, seventy, seventy-one, seventy-two, seventy-three, seventy-four, seventy-five, seventy-six, and seventy-seven, of the Big Muddy Coal and Iron Company's subdivision adjoining the town of Pilot Knob, Iron County, Missouri, and in addition thereto such points of interest as the park commission to be hereinafter named may deem necessary for the purposes of the park and the Secretary of War may approve, the whole containing about one hundred acres and costing not to exceed seven thousand five hundred dollars.

Sec. 2. That the establishment of the Pilot Knob National Military Park shall be carried forward under the control and direction of the Secretary of War; and the Secretary of War shall, upon passage of this Act, proceed to acquire the title to same by voluntary conveyance or under the Act approved August first, eighteen hundred and eighty-eight, entitled "An Act to authorize the condemnation of land for sites for public buildings, and for other purposes," or under the Act approved February twenty-second, eighteen hundred and sixty-seven, entitled "An Act to establish and protect national cemeteries," as he may elect or deem practicable; and when title is procured to all of the lands and roads within the boundaries of the proposed park, as described in section one of this Act, he may proceed with the establishment of the park; and he shall detail an officer of the Engineer Corps of the Army to assist the commissioners in establishing the park.

Sec 3. That the affairs of the Pilot Knob National Military Park shall be subject to the supervision and direction of the Secretary of War, be in charge of three commissioners to be appointed by the Secretary of War, each of whom shall [be veterans of the] troops engaged in the battle of Pilot Knob to enter upon the [missing word(s)] engaged therein, two of whom shall have served in the force commanded by General Ewing and one in the army commanded by General Price. The commissioners shall select one of the number chairman; they shall also elect, subject to the approval of the Secretary of War, a secretary, who shall also be historian, and they and the secretary shall have an office in the town of Pilot Knob, Missouri, or on the grounds of the park, and be paid such compensation as the Secretary of War shall deem reasonable and just.

Sec. 4. That it shall be the duty of the commissioners named in the previous section, under the direction of the Secretary of War, to restore the redoubt known as Fort Davidson and the rifle pits connecting therewith; to open and construct such roads as may be necessary, and to ascertain and mark with historical tablets or otherwise, as the Secretary of War shall determine, the lines of battle of the troops engaged in the assault and the lines and positions held by the troops defending Fort Davidson and the Arcadia Valley during the battle and other historical points of interest pertaining to the assault upon and the defense of Fort Davidson; and the said commissioners in establishing this military park shall also have authority, under the direction of the Secretary of War, to do all things necessary to the purposes of the park and for its establishment under such regulations as the Secretary of War may consider best for the interests of the Government, and he shall make and enforce all needful regulations for the care of the park.

Sec. 5. That it shall be lawful for any State that had troops engaged in the battle of Pilot Knob to enter upon the lands of the Pilot Knob Military Park for the purpose of ascertaining and marking the lines of battle and positions of its troops engaged therein: *Provided,* That before any such lines or positions are permanently marked the designation of the position or lines and the proposed method of marking them by monuments, tablets, or otherwise shall be submitted to and approved by the Secretary of War, and all such lines and positions and the designs and inscriptions for the same shall first receive the written approval of the Secretary of War, which approval shall be based on formal written reports which must be made to him in each case by the commissioners of the park, and no monument or other designating indication shall be erected or placed within said park or vicinity without such written authority of the Secretary of War: *Provided,* That no discrimination shall be made against any State as to the manner of designating lines or positions but any grant made to any State by the Secretary of War may be used by any other State. The provisions of this section shall also apply to organizations and persons.

Sec. 6. That if any person shall, except by the permission of the Secretary of War, destroy, mutilate, deface, injure, or remove any monument, column, statue, memorial structure, tablet, or work of art that shall be erected or placed upon the grounds of the park by lawful authority, or shall destroy or remove any fence, railing, inclosure, or other work intended for the protection or ornamentation of said park or any portion thereof, or shall destroy, cut, bark, hack, break down, or otherwise injure any tree, bush, or shrub that may be growing upon said park, or shall cut down or fell or remove any timber, battle relic, tree or trees growing or living upon said park, or hunt within the limits of said park, or shall remove or destroy any breastworks, earthworks, walls or other defenses or shelter on any part thereof constructed for the defense of this position on the lands or approaches to the park, any person so offending and found guilty thererof before any United States commissioner or court, justice of the peace of the county in which the offense is committed, or any court of competent jurisdiction, shall, for each and every such offense, forfeit and pay a fine, in the discretion of said commissioner or court of the United States or justice of the peace, according to the aggravation of the offense, of not less than five nor more than five hundred dollars, one half for the use of the park and the other half to the informant, to be enforced and recovered before such United States commissioner or court, justice of the peace or other court in like manner as debts of like nature are now by law recoverable in the several counties where the offense may be committed.

Sec. 7. That to enable the Secretary of War to begin to carry out the purpose of this Act, including the purchase or condemnation of the necessary land marking the boundaries of the park, opening or repairing necessary roads, restoring the field to its condition at the time of the battle, maps and surveys, material, labor, clerical and all other necessary assistants, and the pay and expense of the commissioners and their secretary and assistants, the sum of twelve thousand dollars, or such a portion thereof as may be necessary, is hereby appropriated out of any money in the Treasury not otherwise appropriated, and disbursements under this Act shall require the approval of the Secretary of War, and he shall make annual report of same to Congress.

Notes

INTRODUCTION

1. The entire Cyrus Peterson Collection at the Missouri Historical Society contains stories of the battle as well as mentions, letters and information including a ledger of paid members of the Pilot Knob Memorial Association.

CHAPTER 1

2. Colonel Hovey was promoted to Brigadier General September 5,1862. The fort is still officially recognized in Francis Heitman's listing of U.S. Forts as Fort Hovey, not Curtis. It is called Fort Curtis in the Official Records of the War of Rebellion. Francis B. Heitman, *Historical Register and Dictionary of the United States Army: From Its Organization, September 29, 1789 to March 2, 1903*, vol. 2 (Washington, D.C: Government Printing Office, 1903), 510.
3. Scans of the originals for eight issues can be found at http://history. alliancelibrarysystem.com/IllinoisAlive/files/is/htm2/ispicket.cfm. *Normal Picket* 1, no. 3, "Fort Hovey," January 8, 1862, 3, Milner Library, Illinois State University.
4. *Normal Picket* 1, no. 2, "Fort Hovey Nearly Completed," January 1, 1862, 2, Milner Library, Illinois State University.

5. Jack Mayes, who has spent sixty years researching this battle and Iron County history, believes that minimally 2,500 soldiers were consistently stationed here time in 1862–63. The Official Records confirm this number. A postwar report by Captain William Hoelcke, engineer, reports 4,000 stationed here in the early years (see note 49). Jack Mayes, unpublished conversations with author, 2010.

6. *Normal Picket* 1, no. 3, "The Post Bakery," January 8, 1862, 2, Milner Library, Illinois State University; *Normal Picket* 1, no. 3, "The 38th Camp," January 8, 1862, 2, Milner Library, Illinois State University.

7. *Normal Picket* 1, no. 3, "Departure of Hecker's Men," January 8, 1862, 3, Milner Library, Illinois State University.

8. A December 18, 1862 letter from General John Gray to General Carr states that barracks for two companies have been completed a little south of the depot using the long timbers from the old quarters of the 33rd Illinois at Arcadia. John Bradbury, "Unpublished Notes from the National Archives about Pilot Knob RG-393," part 4, 2009, Fort Davidson, Pilot Knob, Missouri; a newspaper article reports: "The rebels fired the iron works, and also burned down the barracks built by Government as quarters for free negroes." *Missouri Republican*, "The Rebel Invasion. Additional from Pilot Knob. News of the Battle Confirmed. Rebels Pass Potosi Going West," October 1, 1864, 1.

9. *Normal Picket* 1, no. 8, "General Calls at This Post," February 12, 1862, 4, Milner Library, Illinois State University.

10. After the Battle of Pilot Knob, Dr. Seymour Carpenter apparently left one of the telegram books he was charged with protecting inside the church. Many of the telegrams, like this one, do not appear in the Official Records. "Telegrams Sent: To Captain Dyer, A.A.G., St. Louis from Colonel John B. Gray, Pilot Knob, 19 Jan 1863" in Immanuel Lutheran Church Book (Pilot Knob, MO, 1863). Also see the January 22, 1863 letter from General Gray to Major Curtis in Bradbury.

11. Grant was promoted to brigadier general on August 5, 1861, and reportedly received notification of this beneath an oak tree on property owned by James Lindsay (colonel, 68th Enrolled Missouri Militia), which is now the Ste. Marie du Lac Roman Catholic Church. Some doubt that he truly received the notification there, but since the soldiers of the 21st Illinois had the monument constructed there (and they could have had it constructed anywhere), it would seem beyond a doubt that the notification that he was indeed a brigadier occurred at that spot.

12. John Kelsey, Letter to Mother Sarah Kelsey 11 Oct 1862 from Camp Curtis (reportedly in Pilot Knob), Accession #65-2006-005-0015, pages 2–3, the Norma Davidson Collection, Fort Davidson State Historic Site. Also, a letter written three days later noted: "There is a good many soldiers here and still a coming it is supposed there will be a move made shortly and it is thought that they march to Little Rock." Private Kelsey apparently could not write, as the spelling, grammar and handwriting changes from letter to letter. Private Kelsey died of pneumonia February 18, 1863, at Jefferson Barracks and is buried in section 39 site 4563. Kelsey, Letter to Mother Sarah Kelsey 14 Oct 1862, Accession #65-2006-005-0016, Norma Davidson Collection, Fort Davidson State Historic Site.

13. Letter from Colonel Commanding to General Davidson dated 22 Apr 1863, in Bradbury.

14. Second Lieutenant W.A. Pollock, description of armaments and supplies, Letter dated 6 June 1863, in Bradbury.

15. James Wilson, Letter to Brigadier General Thomas Ewing from Major Wilson, dated 25 Aug 1864 at Pilot Knob, *The Civil War CD-Rom: The War of the Rebellion: A Compilation of the Official Records of the Union and Confederate Armies*, version 1.5 CD-Rom (Carmel, IN: Guild Press, 1996), series 1, volume XLI/2 (S#84), pages 855–56, CD-Rom page ar84_855.

16. Robert L. Lindsay, "Pilot Knob, Mo.—The Battle Fought There, September 26th and 27th, 1864," *Forge*, October 19, 1865, 1.

17. The 1st Nebraska broke ground on Fort Davidson on June 26, 1863. August Scherneckau, *Marching with the First Nebraska* (Norman: University of Oklahoma Press, 2007), 178–195. General Fisk complains that he has no men who are trained in handling the large guns, which probably generated the idea to train some of the African American "contrabands" to do this task. This served the Union well at the Battle of Pilot Knob. Clinton B. Fisk, Letter to Major General John M. Schofield dated 22 Sep 1863, *The Civil War CD-Rom*, series 1, volume XXII/2 (S#33), pages 567–68, CD-Rom page ar33_567.

18. R.R. Livingston, *Order 29 June 1863*, Missouri Secretary of State (MoSOS) Provost Marshal Records, F1481; Robert Lindsay, Letter to General John Schofield 30 June 1863, MoSOS Marshal Records, F1481; Nebraska Adjutant General Office, 1st Nebraska Cavalry Reel 3, RG18-20410, General Orders #10 dated 30 June 1863.

19. "It would have been better to ask for permission before calling out the citizens to work on forts. Not deemed proper unless in case of urgent necessity that I don't think exists." John Schofield, Letter to Col. Livingston

2 Jul 1863, in Bradbury; another letter complained that a contraband Samuel Carson, his employee, was required to work on Fort Davidson. N.C. Griffith, Letter to Brig. Gen. Clinton Fisk 4 Sep 1863, MoSOS Provost Marshal Records, F1481.

20. The "African Phalanx" consisted of men hired or required by the army to build the fort. Willis Cole, an African American survivor of this battle, reported that "I first knew Moses Lax in the spring of 1863 when we were both located as soldiers at Pilot Knob, or rather he was working there for the government building the Fort." Moses later joined the 62nd U.S. Colored Infantry, Company D, in December 1863 and served until December 1866. Willis Cole, Moses Lax Pension Records: Deposition C by Willis Cole, June 29, 1914 (Washington, D.C.), 14. Also, they were allowed one half-gill per man morning and evening. Galen Baldey, Lieutenant, Letter to Commander 1st Nebraska in Bradbury.

21. Brigadier General Clinton Fisk, Letter to Major General John M. Schofield dated 22 Sep 1863, *The Civil War CD-Rom*, series 1, volume XXII/2 (S#33), pages 567–68, CD-Rom page ar33_567.

22. Captain William Hoelcke, Letter to Major O.D. Greene dated 27 Feb 1864, *The Civil War CD-Rom*, series 1, volume XXXIV/2 (S#62), pages 434–35, CD-Rom page ar62_434.

23. Henry Wilkinson, Letter No. 15, the Cyrus Peterson Collection, Box 8, Folder 4, Missouri Historical Society, St. Louis, Missouri.

24. This is no longer the case, due to fill rock being deposited on the field by the mining company. It appears much more like a flat field than the sloping field it was.

25. This telegram also does not appear in the Official Records of the War of Rebellion. This one reads: "The Small Pox Patients are one half mile west of Iron Mountain Depot [at Middlebrook] in two tents separated at some distance from each other. I forward for post hospital at Ironton today forty four (44) patients." W. Dickinson, "Telegrams Received: To General John Gray dated 9 Mar 1863," Immanuel Lutheran Church Book.

26. Several soldiers spent enough time up there to carve their names in the rocks at the summit. One of the soldier's names I found carved in the rocks was Luther Prosser, 33rd Illinois Infantry. His service record states that he enlisted on September 2, 1861, and mustered out November 24, 1865. He was promoted from private to commissary sergeant during the time. His record states that he was a teacher from Kinmundy, Marion County, Illinois. Illinois Secretary of State, Civil War Soldiers Database (Springfield, Illinois), found at www.sos. state.il.us/departments/archives/datcivil.html#nationalparkservice.

27. *Engraving of Camp Blood*, probably from a drawing by William Henchey, a local artist. Francis B. Heitman, *Historical Register*, 508; Alfred H. Guernsey and Henry M. Alden, *Harper's Pictorial History of the Civil War*, vol.1 (Chicago, IL: McDonnell Bros., 1866), 171.

28. Letter to Colonel Tyler from General Thomas Ewing, on 18 Jun 1864 from St. Louis, *The Civil War CD-Rom*, series 1, volume XXXIV/4 (S#64), page 443, CD-Rom page ar64_443.

Chapter 2

29. Brigadier General Thomas Ewing, "The Late Campaign. The Part Taken by General Ewing and His Command. Gen. Ewing's Official Report. A Deeply Interesting Narrative," *Missouri Democrat*, November 11, 1864, 4.

30. Brigadier General L.C. Hunt, Letters to Lieutenant Colonel C.B. Comstock dated 9 Apr 1864 and 12 Apr 1864, Fort Davidson State Historic Site Archives, Accession #65.2006.002.0001.

31. This letter also reports damp conditions in the powder magazine and that the south rifle pit extended farther past Knob Creek. Lieutenant Amos Stickney, Letter to Major O.D. Greene dated 12 Jul 1864, *The Civil War CD-Rom*, series 1, volume XLI/2 (S#84), pages 146–47, CD-Rom page ar84_146. Stickney's decision to build a fort atop Rock Mountain was not well liked by Captain William Hoelcke. In a letter dated August 22, 1864, written to Colonel O.D. Greene, Hoelcke states: "I reported at the time to Brigadier-General Ewing the fact and was opposed to the construction of any additional work, at least on the mentioned hill…The defenses of Pilot Knob are not in Pilot Knob itself; they are on three points in a circle around the place—First, two miles south in Arcadia; second, one mile and a half east on the Farmington road; third, one mile and a half west on the Caledonia road. This arrangement would scatter a small force too much, and to concentrate the force. Fort Davidson, in the Pilot Knob Valley, had been constructed only against a sudden raid. The place can be held with the present defenses, and more so when the proposals of Captain Gerster are carried out, until re-enforcements arrive." Captain William Hoelcke, Letter to Colonel O.D. Greene dated 22 Aug 1864, *The Civil War CD-Rom*, series 1, volume XLI/2 (S#84), pages 805–6, CD-Rom page ar84_805; following is a letter from Anton Gerster, captain and assistant engineer, to Captain Hoelcke at the

headquarters of the Department of the Missouri, in St. Louis, of August 20, 1864: "In compliance with Special Orders, No. 227, Department of the Missouri, I proceeded at once to Pilot Knob, Mo., and examined the powder magazine in Fort Davidson. I found the powder magazine in pretty good order, but to prevent any dampness for the future it will be well to raise the floor about twelve inches to get room enough for the air to circulate, and also to lead off all water that may settle below the floor. In constructing a drainage from the bottom of the powder magazine, through the parapet into the ditch, will secure to the powder magazine permanent safety. According to your verbal instructions in regard to the newly commenced work on Rocky Hill, right above the railroad depot, I have to report that it is very impracticable. In the first place Pilot Knob post cannot be defended well enough from it in consequence of its height and steepness—so much so that the guns cannot be depressed enough to do any damage to any attacking force. The railroad depot, at the same time the main depot of the quartermaster's department, are close to the foot of the hill. The main object is to hold the depot, and this cannot be done on account of the above-mentioned reason. Being at the depot an enemy is entirely below the range of any fire from the place where the new fort is laid out. The depot will be destroyed, and nothing can prevent it while a garrison is safe in a fort of no purpose whatever but to save itself. On the top of the hill where the new fort is laid out is no material whatever but stone, the most dangerous material for a breast-work. To carry others up is almost impossible, or at least very expensive. With the force on hand to build it in the way it is laid out will take a very long time. A working party of 200 men a day wants about six months to finish it; besides there is no water on the hill, and a well (artesian well), to bore through the stones, possibly, will require a depth of some 500 feet at a cost of not less than $2,500. Fort Davidson, however, with all its faults, against a regular siege, is mainly constructed against a raid until re-enforcements may reach the place and fulfill the purpose, provided the garrison does its duty. To have it, however, strengthened I suggest that a bomb-proof block-house may be erected within the fort. The place d'armée is sufficiently large enough to hold more than 250 men (the reserve) under cover while a regular attack is made. To strengthen the place still more it may be advisable to construct a rifle-pit from the southeast corner of Fort Davidson across the Arcadia road; also one from the northwest corner of the fort in a northerly direction across the Caledonia road. Both lines should be straight, so that they may be enfiladed from the fort."

32. Major James Wilson, Letter to Brigadier General Thomas Ewing dated 25 Aug 1864, *The Civil War CD-Rom*, series 1, volume XLI/2 (S#84), pages 855–56, CD-Rom page ar84-855.

33. St. Mary's Catholic Church was destroyed by a tornado in 1957 and never rebuilt. Henry Wilkinson, Wilkinson Letter No. 15, Cyrus Peterson Collection, Box 8, Folder 4, Missouri Historical Society, St. Louis, Missouri.

34. P.E. McDuffie, Civil War Field Fortifications, Rifle Trench, http:// sites.google.com/site/confedengineerlh/event-vision/civil-war-field-fortifications-website---detailed-notes-on-rifle-pits.

35. There is much speculation to this day as to the number of soldiers in Price's army. Most authorities say twelve thousand (of which five thousand under General Shelby were heading to Potosi at the time of this battle). For the past ten years, I've been compiling lists of soldiers from rosters and currently have more than twenty-one thousand names of Price's army (including operating guerrillas) prior to his debacle at Mine Creek. In my opinion, twelve thousand is a low number for the soldiers under Price. I believe that he entered the state with between fifteen and eighteen thousand men.

36. *Missouri Democrat*, "The Hero of Pilot Knob. Serenade to Gen. Ewing. A Large Turn-Out. Speeches of Mayor Thomas, General Ewing, Major Williams, Hon. C.D. Drake, and Col. Baker," October 8, 1864, 4.

37. *Yonker's Herald*, "General Thomas Ewing's Great Military Feat Fifty Years Ago," September 24, 1914, Ohio Historical Society, Columbus, Ohio, call #PA BOX 419, page 13.

38. Cyrus L. Peterson and Joseph M. Hanson, *Pilot Knob: The Thermopylae of the West* (Independence, MO: Two Trails Publishing, 2000), telegrams addenda, 2.

39. Sherman trusted the opinion of General Thomas Ewing sufficiently to offer him a command on his march to the sea and had him with him while discussing his plans with Grant at Pana, Illinois. His opinion of Tom's brother, Hugh, was that he drank too much, and he considered the youngest Ewing brother, Charles, too much of a gambler—indeed, so much so that he did not support Charles's promotion to brigadier general, which the family pushed through late in the war. For the march to the sea info, see Harrison Hannahs, *General Thomas Ewing, Jr.* (Topeka, KS: State Printing Office, 1912), 276–82, Collections of the Kansas State Historical Society, 1911–12; for the Ewing brothers and their habits, see Stanley P. Hirshson, *The White Tecumseh: A Biography of William T. Sherman* (New York: John Wiley & Sons, Inc., 1997), 8 and 188.

40. Henry Wilkinson, Wilkinson Letter No. 19, Cyrus Peterson Collection, Box 8, Folder 4, Missouri Historical Society, St. Louis, Missouri, circa 1905.

41. Byrce A. Suderow, ed., "Pt. 1 Unpublished Communications Price's Army," Missouri Civil War Message Board, January 20, 2006.

CHAPTER 3

42. *Missouri Democrat*, "Ovation to Col. Tom Fletcher. Serenade at Barnum's Hotel. Speeches of Hon. Henry T. Blow, Col. Fletcher and Maj. Murphy," October 14, 1864.

43. Peterson and Hanson, *Pilot Knob*, 176.

44. *Missouri Democrat*, "The Hero of Pilot Knob."

45. If I were to guess at a more precise location on Dobbins's camp, it would be north of modern-day Shepherd Mountain Road and a few hundred yards west of the 800 block of West Mulberry. According to Robert L. Lindsay's article, "[T]he rebels withdrew out of range of our guns, and began immediately to prepare ladders to scale the walls of the fort" and camped "*apparently* [emphasis added] not over three hundred yards distant." T.J. Mackey, Price's engineer, states that Dobbins camped nine hundred yards from the fort. T.J. Mackey, "A Lady of Arcadia. The Doomed Garrison of Pilot Knob, and How It Was Saved," *Monthly Illustrator and Home and Country* 11, no. 4 (November 1895): 325.

46. "Captain Jim" was the nickname of James Farrar, a local civilian African American who helped man the thirty-two-pound cannon in the fort. He was wounded in the lower abdomen when he and three other African Americans were hit by an exploding shell fired by the Confederates. Both Lieutenant David Murphy and Colonel Fletcher report that he was carried during the retreat to Dr. Carpenter's hospital. Peterson and Hanson, *Pilot Knob*, 172. According to local folklore told by the oldest members of Immanuel Lutheran Church, the late Nell White among them, Farrar was carried to the church and concealed beneath the trapdoor. Laying on the earthen floor below the church in a crawl space, he died the next day.

47. About 250 were eventually rounded up. *Missouri Democrat*, "The Fighting at Pilot Knob. Full and Graphic Details. Assault by Vastly Superior Numbers A Heroic and Glorious Defense," September 30, 1864, 1.

48. Information from a letter from forty-eight German citizens of Pilot Knob who were in the battle. Many of these Germans had much to lose by staying behind, as at least fifteen of them had been part of the "damned

Dutch" home guard at Pilot Knob in 1861. The German citizen-soldiers included Immanuel Luthern Church's new pastor of only three months, Reverend C.A. Gräber. Walter E. Busch, translator, Letter to the Editor, *Westliche Post*, October 8, 1864.

49. Peterson and Hanson, *Pilot Knob*, 181.

50. Private Amos Thomas Long, Company K, 3rd MSM, claims to be in the fort asleep when magazine blew. Family story says that he and another unknown put on Confederate uniforms and stayed with the Rebels three or four days until he could escape. He is not on the company list, and the company muster roll states missing in action, since last muster returned to company. Cyrus A. Peterson, Letter to Thomas Ewing III 29 May 1903, Cyrus Peterson Collection, Box 3, Folder 4, Missouri Historical Society.

51. Moore reports that there was plenty of fire in the magazine and that they didn't need a trail. Some take this to mean he set the fire. Peterson and Hanson, *Pilot Knob*, 182. Sergeant Daniel Flood insistently wrote that he set the match. This could be resolved as Moore's language does not say that he specifically set the fire. So, while it may seem Moore set the fire, it is possible that he is only reporting that it had been set by Flood, who had been detailed to set it. However, since most authorities have Moore setting the fire, I decided not to quibble with that. Peterson and Hanson, *Pilot Knob*, 187–88.

52. *Yonker's Herald*, "General Thomas Ewing's Great Military Feat," 13; Dr. C.A. Peterson, Letter to Thomas Ewing Jr (General's Son), May 29, 1903. A copy is located in Mayes's Collection, Folder #1, Fort Davidson State Historic Site.

53. Henry Clay Thompson II, *The County Historian: First Part of A Short History of St. Francois County* (N.p.: Walsworth Publishing Co., 1992), 90.

54. The thirty-four-star Union flag is now in the possession of the Iron County Historical Society. For years at Pilot Knob Memorial Association anniversary celebrations, it was brought out and displayed for all to see.

55. Hollatz's tombstone states that he was killed in the Battle of Pilot Knob, but he is never listed as being at the battle by any of the survivors. (However, the Germans were largely forgotten by many of the English-speaking survivors.) Peter Allgier Sr. left his family to enter the fort and was never heard from again (he is also not on any lists written by survivors). His son, Peter Jr., led many people to safety in the hills prior to the battle.

56. Major General Sterling Price Court of Inquiry, Examination of Capt. T.J. Mackey, corps of engineers 24 Apr 1865, *The Civil War CD-Rom*, series 1, volume XLI/1 (S#83), page 710, CD-Rom page ar83_710.

57. Ewing, "The Late Campaign," *Missouri Democrat*.

58. Ibid.; Pilot Knob Memorial Association, *Third Annual Meeting of the Pilot Knob Memorial Association* (St. Louis, MO: A.R. Fleming Printing Co., 1906), 3–8.

59. *Missouri Democrat*, "From Pilot Knob. The Rebel Wounded at Ironton Their Dead—The Terrible Punishment Inflicted by Ewing—Rebel Depredations," October 14, 1864, 1.

60. The 10th Kansas came to Pilot Knob to clean up after battle. Two hundred prisoners were to do the work. Transcribed research copy available at Fort Davidson State Historic Site in Folder P17. James A. Smith, Statement of 1st Sergeant James A. Smith, 10th Kansas Veteran Infantry 15 Aug 1906, Cyrus Peterson Collection, Box 6, Missouri Historical Society.

Chapter 4

61. Brigadier General Thomas Ewing, Letter to Colonel Callender dated 17 Oct 1864, *The Civil War CD-Rom*, series 1, volume XLI/4 (S#86), page 37, CD-Rom page ar86_37.

62. Lieutenant Colonel David Murphy, Report of Lieutenant Colonel David Murphy, inspector, District of St. Louis, for December 1864, *The Civil War CD-Rom*, series 1, volume XLVIII/1 (S#101), pages 520–21, CD-Rom page ar101_520.

63. The text concerning Pilot Knob includes the following: "2. Maps of Pilot Knob, Mo. & vicinity. To show a better and clear reading of the topography the standing timber is not represented. In the beginning of the war in 1861, Cape Girardeau, Pilot Knob, Rolla and Jefferson City were the outer line of our defences in this State. I was ordered to strengthen the position of Pilot Knob the terminus of the Iron Mountain & St. Louis Rail Road, which was occupied by a force near or over 4,000 men. I fortified a commanding eminence (afterwards called Fort Curtis) in the Arcadia Valley some three miles south of Pilot Knob also other valuable points in front on the right and left flank to guard the approaches. With the above mentioned force & the Fortifications our position was perfectly secure under an attack of any number. As soon as the current of war changed South by the capture of New Madrid, Island No. 10., The Forts Donelson and Henry and the evacuation of Columbus, there seemed no necessity for having such a large force at Pilot Knob & consequently the number of troops at that point were reduced to a minimum of about 300 men. Fort

Curtis being too far from our Depot of Quarter Master Stores & etc. was abandoned and dismantled, and Fort Davidson erected. If it had been left to me I should have prolonged the Rail Road to the Arcadia Valley and there establish the depot, it is a much better and more defensible position even with a very small garrison against any large attacking party…" and also "Plan of Fort Davidson in the Pilot Knob Valley. The profile of the Fort is the normal profile as it is constructed on level ground with no defilement. The hills surrounding the Fort are about 500 feet high and it would have been useless to defile the fort against such hights [sic] so close to it. On the other hand it would have been equally useless to errect [sic] a Fort on any of those hills. They are so steep and rocky that artillery could not be depressed enough to injure an enemy coming into the valley. All the Roads leading into the valley upon which an enemy would have to come, were well defended by the Fort. The hills are very rocky and almost inaccessible for Armies and have a slope of from 35° to 65°. The Fort was attacked last fall by the Rebels under Price and withstood the first attack handsomely. It could not stand very well a regular attack, it was not built for that purpose, only to hold out against a sudden raid or assault. And as the enemy apparently intended to proceed to a regular siege, and as the time of retreat and reinforcement had been previously cut off by the insurgents, the Fort was evacuated and blown up by our forces during the night following the first attack. After we got possession of Pilot Knob again and I returned to St. Louis with Major General Rosecrans from the pursuit of Price, I made a plan for strengthening the old Fort Davidson shown in the annexed Copy of Plan & Sections of Fort Davidson showing the alteration to strengthen it. In the alteration it is a mere Blockhouse. The destruction of the Fort by the exploding of the Powder Magazine was not effective enough. The parapet was and is still good, only the Magazine was entirely destroyed. Only one of the 32 Pounder barbette guns was upset by the explosion. The Garrison after the retreat of Price was very small and it was useless with so few hands to commence so extensive and laborious a work. Afterwards the surrender of the Rebel Armies made any work useless." Captain William Hoelcke, Letter to Brigadier General R. Delafield, 22 Sep 1865, National Archives Record Group 77, item H 1961, Fort Davidson State Historic Site, Folder U22.

64. *The Pilot Knob Near St. Louis. Um die Welt* (*Around the World*) (N.p.: A Keppler Publication, July 15, 1882), 291. Fort Davidson State Historic Site, Accession #65.2000.011.0001.

CHAPTER 5

65. A clipped article with notation "Rep 4/12/16" on it—probably meaning *Missouri Republican* newspaper for April 16, 1916—mentions David Murphy being commander of the Missouri GAR, but that is not in his official biography. It may be that he was commander, as much of the pre-1880 GAR information is lost, or that he was commander of a St. Louis post. For the record, he is buried in section 4, grave 12476 at Jefferson Barracks National Cemetery, St. Louis, Missouri. "David Murphy, Once Judge in St. Louis, Dies in San Diego," unknown newspaper, Fort Davidson State Historic Site, Folder #U32.

66. By 1917, 594 posts had been at one time or another mustered into the GAR in Missouri. Walter E. Busch, with Vernon Stottlemyre, Douglas Niermeyer and Jeff Henningfield, "Missouri G.A.R. Posts Listings," published in part on the web at http://www.suvcwmo.org/garposts.php.

67. The "Camp-fires of the G.A.R." contains the reminiscences of General William T. Sherman. Various authors, *Life and Reminiscences of General Wm. T. Sherman by Distinguished Men of His Time* (Baltimore, MD: R.H. Woodward Co., 1891), 455–67.

68. See *Second Annual Meeting of the Pilot Knob Memorial Association*, for evidence of using the fort for GAR campfires. Also several records of Memorial Day celebrations in the *Iron County Register* state specifically that the Union church, which was located at the modern-day corner of East Maple and Highway 221 (possibly on some of the current historic site property) was used for the services and special meetings on that day and that campfires were set at night inside the fort.

69. For more information on these Southern memorial organizations and the myth of the Lost Cause, I strongly recommend Gary W. Gallagher and Alan T. Nolan, *The Myth of the Lost Cause and Civil War History* (Bloomington, IN: Indiana University Press, 2000) and William Blair, *Cities of the Dead: Contesting the Memory of the Civil War in the South 1865–1914* (Chapel Hill: University of North Carolina Press, 2004). The United Daughters of the Confederacy were so strong and the myth of the Lost Cause became so implanted in both southern and northern culture that the group could erect monuments, such as the one in Union City, Tennessee, claiming that Southern soldiers died there, thus preserving Anglo-Saxon culture in the South, without being asked a simple question. Since most northerners and most of England were Anglo-Saxon as well, what form of Anglo-Saxon culture did they save?

70. *Confederate Veteran* 8, no. 5 (May 1900): 222.

71. Kirby Ross, ed., *Autobiography of Samuel S. Hildebrand: The Renowned Missouri Bushwhacker* (Fayetteville: University of Arkansas Press, 2005), 241, footnote.

72. This book is a very limited edition, a genealogical bonanza for many of the units involved in the Battle of Pilot Knob. A copy is on file at the Fort Davidson State Historic Site library and the St. Louis Public Library. Geraldine Sanders-Smith, *Civil War Soldiers of Madison County, Missouri and Surrounding Counties* (N.p.: privately published, 1997), 416.

73. Henry Wilkinson's service record is from Sanders-Smith, page 600. "The Great Little Battle " is in the Missouri Historical Society's Cyrus Peterson Collection, Box 8, Folder 3, no date. "Great Little Battle of Pilot Knob," sixty-one pages, original and photocopy. Letter #18 has the same title.

Chapter 6

74. Iron County Recorder of Deeds Office Records, Book 52, 118–27.

75. About August Gehner: He owned August Gehner & Co. in St. Louis. There are two August Gehners listed as Civil War soldiers for the Union. One served in the 1st Missouri Artillery (Backof's Battery) and the other as a bugler in 1st Missouri Cavalry Volunteers, Company B, which was organized in Bunker Hill, Illinois. The correct soldier is probably the one with Backof's Battery, as they were stationed at Pilot Knob for a short time. Iron County Recorder of Deeds Office Records, Book 52, 332–33.

76. Congressman Marion E. Rhodes (1868–1928) attempted at least one bill, according to the text in *Third Annual Meeting* (page 31 of original book, also included here). Other local congressmen, including Politte Elvins, continued working on this project at least through 1909. A copy of H.R. 4923 is in Appendix C.

77. This was still somewhat of a problem in 2001 prior to the Sons of Confederate Veterans finally putting a marker up on the south rifle pit to memorialize their dead. Only the insistence of a few members of the Sterling Price Camp in St. Louis eventually turned the tide, and the Missouri Division of SCV put up the marker. One of the insistent members was Ron Warren of Annapolis. Walter E. Busch, unpublished personal remembrances.

78. W.R. Boggs, Letter to Sterling Price dated 4 Aug 1864, *The Civil War CD-Rom*, series 1, volume XLI/2 (S#84), pages 1040–1041, CD-Rom page ar84_1040.

79. Robert E. Shalhope, *Sterling Price: Portrait of a Southerner* (Columbia: University of Missouri Press, 1971), 262.

80. David Roggensees, former site administrator of Fort Davidson State Historic Site and currently at Nathan Boone State Historic Site near Springfield, has researched this and believes that while Price might not have been a great general, this raid has been very underrated by virtually everyone. Everyone looks at the tactical defeats of Pilot Knob, Westport and the debacle at Mine Creek and considers the entire raid to be a disaster, while David considers it a disaster because the rest of the Confederacy failed to recognize what the Union was being forced to do to combat Price and they failed to act on it. The core ingredients of this argument are also presented in the preface and throughout by Bryce Suderow in *Thunder in the Arcadia Valley* (Cape Girardeau, MO: Center for Regional History and Cultural Heritage, 1986). I use many of David's points, and some that I've added, giving brief talks (one entitled "Did Pilot Knob Save the American Nation?" for instance). However, none of us are of the opinion that the Union would not have ultimately won—only that the war would have been significantly lengthened and elections influenced.

81. Gehner died on May 14, 1910, of myocarditis, with endocarditis contributing to his death. Missouri Bureau of Vital Statistics, Death Certificate #14936. Peterson died on November 19, 1915. The death certificate lists cause of death as paralysis (hemplegia), with senility as a contributory factor. Missouri Bureau of Vital Statistics, Death Certificate #34720.

82. Iron County Recorder of Deeds Office Records, Book 48, pages 327–28.

83. Iron County Recorder of Deeds Office Records, Book 56, page 561.

84. Iron County Recorder of Deeds Office Records, Book 95, page 207.

85. Iron County Recorder of Deeds Office Records, Book 98, 623. Lot 65 transferred separately to the U.S. Forest Service on April 20, 1939. Iron County Recorder of Deeds Office Records, Book 100, page 111.

86. U.S. Forest Service Letter, May 16, 1964, Fort Davidson State Historic Site, Folder #L23.

87. Photo titled "1941 U.S. Forest Service Slide," Fort Davidson State Historic Site, Folder #L38.

88. Photo titled "Fort Davidson, Pilot Knob, Mo., Iron County, On Highway No. 21, See Large Close-up of Sign," dated July 20, 1930. Original owned by Jack Mayes. Fort Davidson State Historic Site, Folder L38.

89. Both sources state that Pilot Knob was defended by General "H.S." Ewing, and Shoemaker credits Sterling Price as being "victorious."

Rader does the better battle description. Both had no problem correctly identifying General Thomas Ewing when talking about "Order No. 11." Floyd C. Shoemaker, *A History of Missouri and Missourians* (Columbia, MO: Walter Ridgway Pub. Co., 1922), 231 and Perry S. Rader, *The History of Missouri: From the Earliest Times to the Present* (Jefferson City, MO: Hugh Stephens Co., 1917), 158.

90. There were several land deals involved in this transfer, including those of a private party. The necessary documents are found in Iron County Recorder of Deeds Office Records, Book 300, pages 706–9, and Book 300, pages 710–11, with the final transferring deed in Book 300, page 712.

Index

A

African Americans 17, 30, 38
African Phalanx 24

B

Battle of Pilot Knob 9, 28, 43, 46,
    47, 56, 59, 66, 67, 70, 71, 76,
    89, 90, 92, 94, 96, 97, 98, 99,
    100, 101, 102, 104, 110, 115,
    117, 119, 125, 127, 138, 139,
    140, 143, 144, 145, 146, 148,
    149, 150, 152, 153, 159, 161,
    165, 166, 167
Big Muddy 51, 52, 166

C

Cabell, William 31, 54, 60, 61, 76,
    146
Cahoon, Benjamin Benson 95, 99,
    108, 123
Campbell, William 36, 60, 61, 68,
    85, 91, 92, 115, 123, 124,
    158, 159, 161, 162
Camp Blood 26

Carlin, W.P. 15, 101, 157
Carpenter, Seymour 33, 35, 74,
    147, 150

D

Dobbins, Archibald 34, 35, 36
Dyer, Daniel B. 41, 88, 108, 109, 123

E

Emerson Park 43, 108
Ewing, Thomas 13, 26, 27, 28, 31,
    32, 33, 34, 35, 36, 37, 38, 39,
    41, 49, 56, 57, 60, 61, 63, 64,
    66, 67, 68, 72, 73, 74, 75, 76,
    77, 78, 81, 98, 99, 101, 103,
    139, 140, 141, 152, 153, 154
    159, 162, 163, 166, 168

F

Fagan, James 54, 60, 61, 72, 98,
    102, 139, 145, 150, 151
Farrar, James 36, 120
1st Missouri 30, 156, 157, 158
1st Nebraska 23, 24, 156, 157, 158

Fisk, Clinton 24, 76, 110

Fletcher, Thomas C. 33, 34, 36, 53, 60, 64, 98, 113, 125, 126, 127, 128, 129, 130, 131, 132, 133, 134, 135, 136, 137, 138

Forest Service 55, 56, 57

Fort Curtis 17, 19, 21, 22, 26

Fort Davidson 9, 13, 14, 15, 17, 23, 24, 25, 26, 28, 29, 31, 33, 38, 42, 46, 52, 55, 56, 57, 66, 67, 68, 69, 71, 94, 96, 98, 115, 118, 122, 127, 140, 141, 146, 150, 151, 159, 161, 162, 163, 167

Fort Hovey 15, 17

47th Missouri Infantry 13, 26, 28, 49, 60, 61, 125, 158, 161

14th Iowa 14, 36, 60, 61, 68, 79, 92, 119, 120, 122, 143, 158, 161

Fredericktown 15, 26, 47, 55, 72, 100, 101, 102, 103, 140, 145, 148, 163

G

GAR 45, 46, 47, 114, 115, 123

Gehner, August 52, 54, 55, 122, 123

Grand Army of the Republic 45, 109, 114

Grant monument 43

Grant, Ulysses S. 19, 26, 43, 46, 102, 104, 107, 108, 109, 141, 155

Great Little Battle 67

H

Hoelcke, William 24, 42, 156

Hunt, L.C. 27, 28

I

Immanuel Lutheran Church 33, 36

iron company 33, 39

Iron Mountain 19, 21, 25, 42, 64, 72, 102, 117, 136, 154, 158

Ironton 15, 17, 22, 23, 25, 31, 32, 38, 46, 55, 59, 62, 70, 74, 80, 85, 94, 102, 108, 143, 146, 147, 148, 152, 161, 164

J

Johnson, T.W. 42, 146, 147, 149, 150

L

Leasburg 57, 67, 68, 75, 76, 92, 98, 99, 159, 161, 162

Lindsay, Robert L. 23

M

Mackey, T.J. 39, 146, 150

Marmaduke, John S. 21, 23, 31, 45, 46, 60, 61, 62, 72, 73, 75, 76, 98, 102, 139, 145, 151

Meloan, William A. 69, 70, 79, 84, 86

Middlebrook 25, 157

Milks, H.B. 37, 38, 67, 85, 86, 91, 123, 124, 142, 159, 162

Mine Creek 53

Mineral Point 33, 34, 72, 101, 102

Murphy, David 31, 41, 45, 54, 60, 61, 68, 69, 70, 77, 78, 80, 81, 83, 84, 85, 87, 91, 93, 94, 95, 96, 100, 101, 102, 103, 104, 105, 109, 110, 112, 116, 119, 123, 124, 139, 140, 142, 144, 148, 149, 153, 158, 161, 162, 163

N

Nifong, Alexander 100–01

P

Pilot Knob Memorial Association
9, 14, 51, 65, 70, 84, 89, 93,
115, 118, 137, 153, 159, 162
Potosi 34, 36
Potosi-Caledonia 33, 34
Price, Sterling 13, 26, 29, 30, 31,
33, 38, 41, 46, 52, 53, 54, 56,
57, 60, 61, 63, 64, 66, 68, 72,
73, 75, 76, 77, 78, 81, 82, 90,
98, 99, 100, 101, 102, 104,
109, 110, 127, 139, 140, 143,
144, 145, 146, 148, 149, 150,
152, 153, 161, 162, 163, 166

R

Rhodes, M.E. 94, 138, 165
Rolla, Missouri 60, 64, 72, 99, 122,
140, 159, 160, 162
Rosecrans, W.S. 59, 60, 64, 72

S

17th Illinois 64, 155, 158
Shelby, J.O. 23, 32, 46, 47, 61, 63,
72, 74, 75, 76, 99, 101, 102,
139, 145, 151
Sherman, William Tecumseh 26,
42, 46, 53, 71, 72, 76
Slayback, Alonzo 31, 32, 33, 34,
151

T

10th Kansas 147, 158
21st Illinois 19, 43, 155
24th Illinois 17, 155

troops killed at Battle of Pilot Knob
39, 63, 66, 74, 93, 98, 102,
119, 144, 146, 147, 148, 149,
150, 151, 152, 153, 162, 163

U

United Daughters of the
Confederacy 46, 52

W

Westport 53, 76
Wilkinson, Henry C. 24, 43, 49,
85, 88, 91, 93, 117, 119, 123,
124, 142, 159, 160, 161, 162,
163
Wilson, James 46, 60, 61, 80, 81,
101, 112, 122, 162
Wilson's Creek 52, 138, 141, 153

About the Author

Walter E. Busch is the natural resources manager for Fort Davidson State Historic Site, Dillard Mill State Historic Site and Elephant Rocks State Park. Walt instructs history, political science and criminal justice part time at Mineral Area College, Park Hills, Missouri. For thirty-two years he was a police officer in Missouri and Illinois and was a police academy instructor for ten years. His bachelor of arts degree was from Tarkio College in criminal justice management and his master of arts degree in humanities with a history emphasis was from California State University–Dominguez Hills. He is the author of several technical documents for the State of Missouri and also of some short articles. His thesis about General Thomas Ewing has been previously published as *General, You Have Made the Mistake of Your Life* and *Myths & Mistakes: The Life of General Thomas Ewing.*

Visit us at
www.historypress.net